McGRAW-HILL PROBLEMS SERIES IN GEOGRAPHY
Geographic Approaches to Current Problems:
the city, the environment, and regional development

Edward J. Taaffe, Series Editor

Wilfrid Bach
AIR POLLUTION

Kevin R. Cox
CONFLICT, POWER, AND POLITICS
IN THE CITY: A Geographic View

Richard L. Morrill and Ernest H. Wohlenberg
THE GEOGRAPHY OF POVERTY in the United States

Harold M. Rose
THE BLACK GHETTO: A Spatial Behavioral Perspective

David M. Smith
THE GEOGRAPHY OF SOCIAL WELL-BEING IN THE UNITED STATES:
An Introduction to Territorial Social Indicators

CONFLICT, POWER AND POLITICS IN THE CITY:
A GEOGRAPHIC VIEW

KEVIN R. COX
Department of Geography
The Ohio State University

McGRAW-HILL BOOK COMPANY
New York   St. Louis   San Francisco   Düsseldorf   Johannesburg
Kuala Lumpur   London   Mexico   Montreal   New Delhi   Panama
Rio de Janiero   Singapore   Sydney   Toronto

1 2 3 4 5 6 7 8 9 0 **DODO** 7 9 8 7 6 5 4 3 2

Library of Congress Cataloging in Publication Data

Cox, Kevin R., 1939-
   Conflict, Power, and Politics in the City

   (McGraw-Hill Problems Series in Geography)
   1. Metropolitan areas—United States. 2. Metropolitan
government—United States. I. Title.
NT334.U5C68   301.5'92   72-6644
ISBN 0-07-013272-0   (pbk.)
ISBN 0-07-013273-9

This book was set in Baskerville by John T. Westlake Publishing
Services. The editor was Janis Yates; the designer was John T. Westlake
Publishing Services; and the production supervisor was Sally Ellyson.

The printer and binder was R. R. Donnelley & Sons Company.
Cover Photographs Courtesy *UPI* and *Trenton Times.* _____

To my parents

CONTENTS

Editor's Introduction   *ix*

Preface   *xi*

Acknowledgements   *xiii*

Chapter 1: Urban Conflict: Theoretical Basis and Resolution

Externality Effects and Locational Conflict   2
The Resolution of Locational Conflict   5
A Paradigm of Locational Conflict and Conflict Resolution   14
The Organization of the Book   15

Chapter 2: The Territorial Organization of Metropolitan Areas

De Facto Territorial Organization   17
De Jure Territorial Organization   20
Territorial Organization of Metropolitan Areas:
    An Integrated View   24
Summary and Concluding Comments   25

Chapter 3: Metropolitan Fragmentation and Urban Conflict

Fiscal Disparities: A General View   28
Fiscal Disparities: The Case of Education   31
Fiscal Disparities: A Quantitative Evaluation   37
An Analysis of the Fiscal Disparities Problem   48
The National Context   48
The Metropolitan Context   51
Summary and Concluding Comments   68

Chapter 4: Conflict and Public Allocation within the City

The Private Component of Environmental Quality	71
The Public Component of Environmental Quality	74
The Public Component of Environmental Quality and Private Investment Decisions	83
The Public Allocation Mechanism	88
Urban Power Structures	97
Summary and Concluding Comments	103

Chapter 5: Policy Implications

Changes in Spatial Organization	107
De Jure Territorial Organization	108
The Distribution of Households and Public Facilities	114
Territorial Organization, Households, and Public Facilities	122
Changes in the Redistribution of Private Resources	125
Summary and Concluding Comments	129
Selected Bibliography	133

EDITOR'S INTRODUCTION

Kevin Cox brings a strong background in the social and behavioral sciences to the geographic study of urban power and conflict. He has been thorough in his examination of the relevant literature in political science, sociology, and economics; and discriminating in his selection of the works in that literature on which to draw.

Professor Cox is particularly penetrating in his analysis of the role of externalities in the distribution of urban power and conflict. Much attention has been given to externalities recently as geographers and other social scientists have recognized that each locational change in a tightly interdependent metropolitan system sets off a complex set of reactions and counterreactions. It is clear that there are such chain effects, but it is by no means clear just what they are. Professor Cox provides a critical breakdown of several types of externalities and their effects. He clearly demonstrates the utility of geography in the study of urban power and conflict in his discussion of the importance of such geographic concepts as distance-decay, perception, and regionalization in establishing the context in which locational externalities express their influence on the city. Distance-decay is evident in the tendency for positive or negative externalities associated with different activities to decline at different rates with distance. The perception of externalities associated with public behavior or status may vary from positive to negative according to the value systems of affected groups. Regionalization is evident in the de facto groupings according to income or race created by the multiplier effects associated with most externalities. A de jure regionalization is the basis for the central-city–suburban fiscal disparities problem, which is dealt with effectively by Professor Cox. He carefully documents the basic contradictions between relatively high per capita demand for services in the central city, compared with the suburb and relatively low per capita tax revenue in the central city, and proceeds to discuss the many ramifications of this contradiction.

Conflict, Power and Politics in the City: A Geographical View is closely related to two other books in the Problem Series—*The Black Ghetto* by Harold Rose and *The Geography of Poverty* by Richard L. Morrill and Ernest H. Wohlenberg. Underling problems of racial conflict and persistent poverty are among the multiplier effects of externalities and the inequalities of power distribution in the city discussed in this volume. Professor Cox tells us what some of the relevant externalities and power distributions are and provides us with a thoughtful consideration of some possible policy alternatives.

This volume will be a useful adjunct to an introductory course stressing geography as a social science, in that it shows how a geographic perspective can provide new insights into some of the city's familiar social problems. It may also provide a useful addition to urban geography courses, as well as to urban-oriented courses in such fields as sociology and political science.

EDWARD J. TAAFFE

PREFACE

That the city has become the prime focus of most of the domestic political issues of the Western world is a fact which does not need extensive documentation. Racial tensions and riots, the virtual bankruptcy of many municipalities, inequalities of wealth, and the increasing role of the government in the urban economy have brought the city into the political forum to a much greater extent than at any time in the past. This is obviously reflected in the platforms of political parties where issues of urban housing, welfare, and pollution assume a growing prominence.

For the geographer, major interest attaches to the fact that many of these political issues have a very strong locational component. That cities vary in their tax bases and in their abilities to supply the needs of their citizens is a striking denial of the egalitarian philosophy in the context of which Western governments operate. Such contrasts are, of course, expressed very strongly in conflicts between localities—as in the fervent desire of poor inner cities for political integration with their less-than-enthusiastic suburban municipalities. Clearly, the locational policies of city governments exercise a potent effect on the ability of the national government to provide the good life for all its citizens—the restrictive residential zoning practices of many suburbs are a case in point.

The locational element in the urban political problem—or problems—of course, has not gone unnoticed by politicians and it is reflected in the policies which they propose. School busing policies, for example, are conceived from an ideological stance in an effort to correct the inequality of educational opportunity. Likewise, the location of new industries in black ghettos is seen as a possible answer to the flight of employment opportunities to the suburbs away from a social group notoriously underprivileged in terms of transportation.

Given this context, this extended essay attempts to place the political problems of the city in a locational perspective. What are the locational patterns which social and territorial conflict assume in the city? What is the locational pattern of the governmental impact which so critically affects the quality of the environment in which we live? What is it about political structures—municipal fragmentation, for example—which produces such variations in the quality of the environment for people in a metropolitan area? And where is power located in the city? Is slum apathy and suburban activism one plausible explanation for the locational problems which beset the urban scene?

These are some of the questions, some of them specific and many of them general, which we confront in this volume. It would be utopian to think that we can propose solutions on the basis of our analysis. The locational problems and locational consequences of policies weave too intricate a web for that to be possible. All we can hope to do is inform. To be aware of the problems and of their complexity may induce some sensitivity in a citizenry which has shown as yet precious little tolerance for the other point of view.

KEVIN R. COX

ACKNOWLEDGMENTS

The following figures and tables are adapted from copyrighted works. The author and publisher express their thanks for permission to use this material.

Table 2.1: Basic Books, Inc. for Table 7-2 from Dick Netzer, *Economics and Urban Problems* (New York: Basic Books, c. 1970), p. 172.

Table 2.2: The Brookings Institution for Table 3-8 from Dick Netzer, *Economics of the Property Tax* (Washington, D.C.: The Brookings Institution, c. 1966), p. 52.

Figure 4.1: Transaction, Inc. for two figures from Theodore J. Lowi, "Apartheid, U.S.A.," *TRANS-action,* February, 1970.

CHAPTER 1

URBAN CONFLICT: THEORETICAL BASIS AND RESOLUTION

The American city is in a state of crisis. The melting pot of yesterday has become a Pandora's box of troubles—flight to the suburbs, ghetto poverty, racial conflict, inadequacies in public provision are fodder for contemporary urban politics. Conflict has become endemic in the metropolitan areas: conflict between the "turfs" of social groups, between suburbs and central city, and between neighborhoods and the city itself. This book is concerned with the geography of these conflicts.

First, what are the *geographic* dimensions of conflict in the city? Which localized populations see themselves as deprived by which other localized populations? Second, why have these conflicts emerged? What are the forces which have generated the conflicts between localized populations? And third, which feasible policies are likely to ameliorate the geographic inequalities lying at the root of the urban crisis.

In brief, this book aims to describe and explicate the nature of the conflicts between localized urban populations. The book offers also a prescription for the solution of these conflicts. However, to order our knowledge in an analytically fruitful manner, we need a set of basic concepts with which we can approach the general topic of locational conflict. These basic concepts form the focus for the remainder of this chapter.

We begin by assuming a purely private economy in which the *individual* decision-making units are households, firms, schools, churches, etc. Each individual decision-making unit has a utility function wherein preferences for various commodity bundles are specified. The word commodity is viewed here in a particularly broad sense and includes such goods and services as clean air, quiet, education, neighborhood quality, and freedom from fear.

In addition, each individual decision-making unit has a set of resources (labor, capital, land, etc.) to be allocated toward securing preferred

1

commodities. Each resource has institutionally protected rights of use associated with it specifying the purposes to which it can or cannot be applied. For example, land in some areas of the city may be used only for residential purposes while in another sector it may be used for either residential or commercial purposes. Such rights are often referred to as "property rights."

Each individual unit attempts to allocate its resources to maximize utility. To achieve this goal, the total net benefits from each activity to which resources are allocated must be maximized. In terms of marginal theory, the individual unit will continue to allocate resources to a given activity until the utility gained from the last unit allocated equals the utility lost from expending resources on that activity rather than on some other activity.

Externality Effects and Locational Conflict

EXTERNALITY EFFECTS

A major factor distorting this theoretical allocational process is that individual utilities are not independent of the resource allocations of others. In contrast to the perfectly competitive private economy used as a theoretical norm in economics, the utility of one individual is very much influenced by the resource allocations of other individuals. These influences are called "externality effects" and are very important to the analysis pursued in this book.

An externality effect exists if an allocation by one individual affects the utility of some other individual. The allocational behavior of whites to keep blacks out of their neighborhoods provides whites with utility but for blacks disutility. In like manner, the use of rivers and streams as dumps for industrial effluent allows the industrial corporation to maximize its utility; but that same behavior imposes disutilities on those who fish and bathe downstream from the industrial plant.

On the other hand, the utilities realized from a mass transit system may be far in excess of those obtained by the city transit authority alone. Health care facilities become more accessible to ghetto residents, thereby decreasing the probability of contagious disease in the city as a whole. Suburban employment opportunities become more accessible to lower-income, central-city residents, a number of whom may obtain steady and well-paying work, thus reducing the city's welfare expenditure while increasing the tax base. It is on the basis of such externality effects that public support of urban mass transit systems is often justified.

Externality effects or, as they are often called, "spillover effects" therefore can take a variety of forms. On the one hand an individual's allocational behavior can provide utilities for others; these externalities are commonly called "positive externalities" or "positive spillovers." As suggested above, a mass transit system has a very wide variety of positive externality effects for an urban population. Positive externalities also are called "indirect benefits."

On the other hand, allocational behavior can provide "disutilities" for others as in the industrial effluent case mentioned above. These externality effects are known as "negative externality" or "negative spillover effects." Negative externalities also can be referred to as "indirect costs."

However not only are indirect costs and benefits important for individual welfare, they are also significant for the efficient allocation of resources for society as a whole. Since the individual decision maker allocates his resources to maximize utility for himself, the effects of his allocation on the utility of others are not considered. Consequently *indirect costs tend to be overproduced* while *indirect benefits tend to be underproduced.* Externality effects, therefore, detract from overall social welfare and pose serious problems for society as a whole as well as for the individuals making up that society.

EXTERNALITY EFFECTS IN A LOCATIONAL CONTEXT

For the geographer considerable interest stems from the fact that externality effects are not spatially random. Rather their intensity is often a function of relative location: this is indicated by the term "neighborhood effects" which is occasionally applied to externalities. As Harvey has shown, factors determining accessibility (nearness, channels, barriers) are all related to the intensity of indirect costs and indirect benefits.[1] For example, the social undesirable imposes the greatest disutilities on his *immediate* neighbors; less disutilities on neighbors at one remove and so forth. Likewise, the houses closer to the factory chimney are likely to suffer more from the disutilities of soot and fumes than houses further from the factory.

Similar locational predictabilities apply to cases of positive externalities: employment opportunities obviously are more available the closer one resides to such opportunities; and indirect benefits provided by a city park decline with decreasing accessibility to the park. It seems valid, therefore, for Tullock to conclude that "the typical externality is 'geographic'."[2]

Assuming a relationship between the intensity of an external effect and relative location, one can deduce easily that in a specifically urban context both the sum of indirect costs and the sum of indirect benefits will tend to be magnified. Within the city, locators are so geographically close to one another that externality-producing allocational behavior is bound to have greater effects on the utilities of others than in a context where population densities are lower. One would anticipate, therefore, that much of the allocational activity within the city would be devoted to minimizing the indirect costs experienced and maximizing the direct benefits received.

The concept of "environmental quality" is also closely related to the indirect costs and benefits impinging upon a locator. Most would agree that there are sharp contrasts in degree of environmental quality of different locations within a typical city. Much of this variation can be

---

[1] David W. Harvey, "Social Processes, Spatial Form and the Redistribution of Real Income in an Urban System," in M. Chisholm, A. Frey and P. Haggett (eds.), *Regional Forecasting,* London: Butterworth, 1971, pp. 273-274.

[2] Gordon Tullock, *Private Wants, Public Means,* New York: Basic Books, 1970, p. 64.

attributed to the externality effects resulting from the allocational activities of others. "Nice" neighborhoods, therefore, are nice partly because other residents engage in preferable forms of public behavior. "Bad" neighborhoods are bad because some of the residents engage in forms of public behavior which impose disutilities. Other aspects of environmental quality can be attributed to the externalities resulting from the allocational activity of local government; for example, a neighborhood may be especially attractive due to vigilance in adhering to local housing codes and zoning regulations.

Externalities, therefore, are crucially important for environmental quality and for the satisfactions which locators experience in different parts of the city. Further, these satisfactions are partly an indirect as well as a direct result of externality effects. For example, externality effects exercise an impact upon the private allocational activities of the individual. The ownership of property in a crime-ridden area of the city necessitates increased expenditures on property insurance or on the interest on loan capital for property renovation purposes.

More generally a high quality environment resulting from a net balance of positive externalities will be reflected in a bidding up of residential property prices in the area: an increase in property values which can be converted into private income via the sale of the property or its rental. Conversely, lower property values are likely to prevail in urban locations having less attractive environments.

The characteristic forms of interdependence between the externality producer and the externality consumer are varied. In some cases, the externalities which locators impose on each other are reciprocal in character. For example, Davis and Whinston have discussed the case where adjacent owners impose costs on each other by underinvesting in the improvement of their properties.[3] In other cases the interdependence may be asymmetrical in character: the smoking factory chimney is a case in point. Figure 1.1 provides a classification of the types of interdependency

Fig. 1.1 Types of interdependency between externality-producing locators.

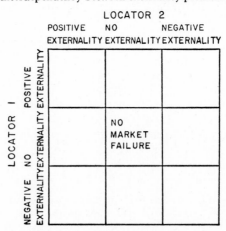

LOCATOR 2

	POSITIVE EXTERNALITY	NO EXTERNALITY	NEGATIVE EXTERNALITY
LOCATOR 1 POSITIVE EXTERNALITY			
NO EXTERNALITY		NO MARKET FAILURE	
NEGATIVE EXTERNALITY			

[3] Otto A. Davis and Andrew B. Whinston, "Economic Problems in Urban Renewal," in E. S. Phelps (ed.), *Private Wants and Public Needs,* New York: W. W. Norton, 1965.

which may relate two locators at a specific location. For each of the two locators, three possible actions are envisaged: providing indirect benefits, producing no externalities or, alternatively, imposing indirect costs. Excluding the case of "no market failure," this produces eight cases of interdependence. These reduce to five when the symmetry of the matrix is taken into account.

Clearly, the existence of externalities poses problems for individual utility-maximizing behavior. The problem can be conceptualized as one of "locational conflict." On the one hand the problem is a conflict between the optimizing goals of the locator and the externality-creating resource allocations of others. On the other hand, the conflict is locational since the magnitude of the externalities is to a high degree a function of the spatial juxtaposition of resource allocators. Consequently, the resultant conflicts call for resolution strategies which are also locational in nature.

The Resolution of Locational Conflict

Locational conflicts involve conflicts between locators and their environment. That environment is created by the allocational behavior of neighboring locators. Conflict resolution, therefore, requires coordination of the activities of the individual with those of the other locators. Such coordination can take place by purely private initiatives or, alternatively, it may have to be pursued through some public mechanism involving coercion by a centralized collective decision-making organization (i.e., a government). First, we consider private methods of coordination and then examine public intervention as a method of coordination of allocations having externality effects.

PRIVATE COORDINATION

Theoretical Alternatives. We have an environment in which externalities are pervasive and in which the individual is not maximizing his utility. Theoretically, there are two broad alternative courses of private action which will move him closer to a private maximum: (1) the individual may alter his environment by relocating to a different environment; i.e., a "relocation strategy"; or (2) the individual may alter his environment by bargaining with those who contribute to (or detract from) its quality; i.e., a "private bargaining strategy." Neither strategy alters existing rights governing the use of property.

In its most basic form the first type of strategy calls for either an "approach" or an "avoid" strategy. This idea may be illustrated by structuring each of the eight types of interdependency discussed above in the form of a game in which strategies are relocational (see Figure 1.2). In Figure 1.2, A and B are locations which can be selected by either of the two locators. Payoffs are hypothetical and of purely heuristic value. The first payoff in each cell refers to the first locator and the second payoff to the second locator.

Two types of games are represented in Figure 1.2. The games in boxes 1, 2, 4, 5, 7, 8 are games of coordination while the games in boxes 3 and 6 are games of conflict. As indicated above there is symmetry in the matrix so that strictly speaking there are three games of coordination and one of conflict.

Fig. 1.2 Private coordination by locational strategy: A and B are locations which can be selected by either of the two locators; payoffs are of heuristic value only, the first payoff in each cell referring to locator No. 1 and the second payoff referring to locator No. 2.

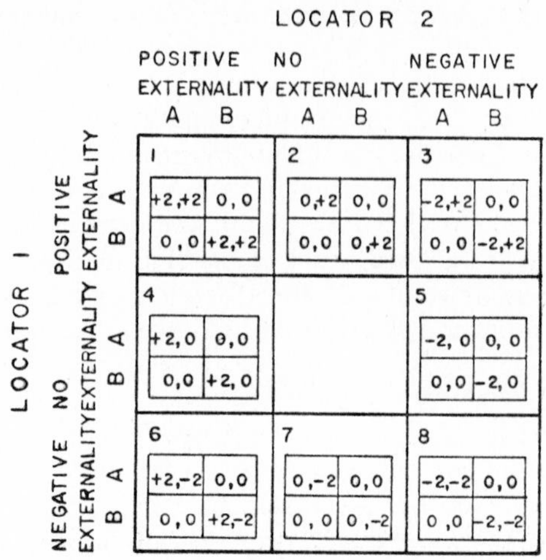

LOCATOR 2

		POSITIVE EXTERNALITY		NO EXTERNALITY		NEGATIVE EXTERNALITY	
		A	B	A	B	A	B
LOCATOR 1 POSITIVE EXTERNALITY	A	**1** +2,+2	0,0	**2** 0,+2	0,0	**3** −2,+2	0,0
	B	0,0	+2,+2	0,0	0,+2	0,0	−2,+2
NO EXTERNALITY	A	**4** +2,0	0,0			**5** −2,0	0,0
	B	0,0	+2,0			0,0	−2,0
NEGATIVE EXTERNALITY	A	**6** +2,−2	0,0	**7** 0,−2	0,0	**8** −2,−2	0,0
	B	0,0	+2,−2	0,0	0,−2	0,0	−2,−2

In the games of coordination, there are obviously strategies which are socially optimal in the sense that one solution makes at least one locator better off without making the other one worse off (i.e. the economist's criterion of Pareto optimality). For example, in game No. 1 in the top left-hand corner, both locators gain by locating in the same place. In game No. 8 in the bottom right-hand corner both locators gain by locating in different places. In game No. 2 locator B is better off by locating at the same place as A; such a choice does not reduce A's utility.

In the games of conflict, on the other hand, there are no such socially optimal solutions. In game No. 6, for example, if the locators choose the same location one gains and the other loses; if they choose different locations one loses and the other gains. This is a little like the problems posed by middle-class movement within a metropolitan area. If the middle-class household stays in the central city the lower class gains from increased central-city tax revenues; the middle-class household loses, however, from exposure to crime and relatively poor schools. On the other hand, the middle-class shift to a suburban municipality imposes a loss on the remaining lower-class households in the form of a reduction in central-city tax revenue.

As a theoretical alternative to relocation utilities may be increased *within the context of the same location* by bargaining between locators. The beneficiary or the loser from the externality may be able to bribe the producer of the externality to adjust his activity to a preferred level; this could be achieved by offering some form of compensation. If a householder does not maintain his residential property adequately so that it detracts from the aesthetic pleasure afforded a neighboring household, the latter might conceivably offer to pay half the bill for a paint and exterior repair job. In an important sense the household would be attempting to transfer some of its neighbor's property rights to itself: in exchange for monetary compensation the household would obtain some of the right to say how the neighboring property could be used. Clearly, there is a tremendous variation in the degree to which such property rights might be transferred: at one end of the theoretical continuum, one can conceive of zero transfer; at the other extreme one can envisage complete transfer of property rights by outright purchase. The latter extreme is characteristic of the strategies employed by universities when they eliminate an important form of negative externality which adjacent land users pose by the consumption of land required for expansion.

The Empirical Outcome. Empirically, however, it is apparent that in private coordination relocational strategies are preferred to bargaining; both the much publicized flight to the suburbs and the population composition turnover of neighborhoods in response to some immediate threat or benefit available elsewhere provide evidence of this. There are at least three reasons for this observed pattern of preference; these reasons refer to the respective opportunity costs of bargaining and relocation and to the degree of facilitation afforded by the private economy.[4]

The opportunity costs of bargaining solutions tend to be high. The bribee is in the position of a monopolist selling part of his property rights to the briber. Due to the locational fixity of the problem, the bribee does not compete in the sale of his property rights. The briber, therefore, will be subject to monopolistic exploitation. Such monopolistic exploitation is not feasible in relocation where sellers of residential properties compete with one another.

Furthermore, due to the absence of a known market price in a monopoly situation, lengthy bargaining will be required. Such bargaining is not costless. In the urban environment in which externalities are pervasive, bargaining will most likely have to be multilateral and under these circumstances bargaining costs assume very large proportions. The greater the number of parties involved in the bargaining, for example, the greater the costs involved in securing agreement on the appropriate level of compensation.

Of particular significance in this context is the problem of "strategic bargaining." As the multilaterality of bargaining increases so the opportunities for holding out for a disproportionately large share of the compensation increase. This is particularly apparent in the land assembly problem where a locator attempts to transfer to himself, by purchase, property rights over a large block of contiguous parcels. For example, if the locator is a university attempting to secure adjacent parcels of land for expansion, success of the project is contingent upon purchase of all parcels of land occupying the space for which the new university building is planned. The individual parcel owner is in the position of a monopolist hoarding a vital resource. If he refuses to sell his plot of land, then the parcels necessary for the construction of the university building cannot be assembled. Under such circumstances, the parcel owner may refuse to sell until offered a price considerably in excess of the price obtainable in a

---

[4] The opportunity costs of the strategy chosen are equal to the benefits foregone by the loss of the opportunity to allocate the resources in other ways.

perfectly competitive land market. The problems created in the form of strategic bargaining where there are many parcel owners can easily be imagined.

In contrast to the high opportunity costs of bargaining solutions, the opportunity costs of relocational solutions tend to be low. Relocation occurs anyway for reasons other than those related to local externalities: job changes, life cycle changes, etc. At such times the opportunity cost of relocation for externality reasons is zero.[5]

Finally, there is a third broad consideration concerning the relative attractiveness of private coordination by relocation; this is the response of the private market economy. Goods and services facilitating a relocational response tend to be supplied; those facilitating a private bargaining response which falls short of outright purchase of property rights tend to be provided at unsatisfactorily suboptimal levels if at all. With respect to relocation, there is the real estate market and, possibly of equal significance, the residential development homogeneous in terms of the income groups it is designed to attract. By appealing to a particular income group the residential developer can help to minimize the presence of individuals imposing those negative externalities which result from budgetary constraint.

On the other hand, there are important logical reasons for anticipating market failure in the supply of bargaining. Bargaining involves the investment of resources from which it is hoped there will be some gains from trade. Money will be traded by the briber for a reduction in the level of indirect costs imposed by, or for an increase in the indirect benefits provided by, the bribee. However, given the externality nature of the problem these gains from trade will take the form of what the economists refer to as "a public good." Public goods are equally available to all with no exclusion. If a resident invests resources in coming to an agreement with a neighbor regarding levels of property maintenance, the benefits from that investment of resources in bargaining (i.e., improved property) will be available to all other residents in the immediate locality and it will be difficult to exclude them from enjoying those benefits. Theoretically, therefore, the individual locator's interest lies in not bargaining at all but in receiving those gains from trade which result from the bargaining efforts of others. Logically, the adoption of this rational strategy by all decision makers results in no bargaining at all. This is known as the "free-rider problem."

In sum, two broad strategies of individual coordination in the externality environment are suggested. The first theoretical alternative is relocational and the second is a private bargaining solution in which the property rights of one locator are transferred in whole or in part to another in exchange for a monetary payment. Empirically, locational solutions appear to be predominant. This is related to the relative opportunity costs of bargaining and relocational solutions respectively and to provision of goods and services upon which the two solutions depend

---

[5] A response frequently encountered in studies of white flight is: "We were thinking of moving anyway." This may be much more plausible than many imagine.

by the private economy. Given the prevalence of relocational solutions, however, what does this suggest about resulting locational patterns?

The Spatial Product of Private Coordination. The result of private coordination using relocational strategies is a set of *de facto territories*. In these territories, individual locators share their positive externalities with one another and are able to avoid those who impose negative externalities. Within metropolitan areas, these take the concrete form of a spatial organization of households into a set of discrete neighborhoods; each neighborhood is homogeneous with respect to income and race. This assumes that income and race are widely perceived as accurate indicators of the type and magnitude of externality effects. This assumption is not difficult to sustain. It is easy to see, therefore, why socially and racially homogeneous residential neighborhoods emerge within a city as a result of residential choice behavior.

The Welfare Implications of Private Coordination. Important questions concern the degree to which de facto territorial organization of the city permits individuals to maximize their own utilities and therefore for social welfare (the sum of individual utilities) to be maximized. It should be emphasized that relocational strategies do not alter the allocational behavior of those producing indirect benefits or indirect costs. Relocation does not induce locators to increase production of indirect benefits or to decrease production of indirect costs simply because it does not alter their property rights in any way. It merely alters the degree to which others experience these indirect costs and benefits by altering their locations with respect to producers.

Within neighborhoods, for example, externalities continue to exist and the allocative decisions of the private individuals producing them take no cognizance of such externalities. For example, individuals continue to invest money in property maintenance at levels which do not reflect the benefits accruing to others in the neighborhood.

Similar problems exist between territories. This is evident in real world analogues of both games of coordination and of conflict. As Harvey has pointed out, for example, in games of coordination there is still the problem of interactions along the boundary between territories occupied by those sharing positive externalities and avoiding the negative externalities imposed by groups in other territories.[6] In games of conflict, on the other hand, relocational strategies adopted by those on whom negative externalities are being imposed merely result in a reallocation of negative externalities.

Middle-class whites in central city neighborhoods, for instance, provide positive externalities for lower-income groups in adjacent neighborhoods. These externalities take specific forms: middle-class groups tend to be less prone to violent forms of public behavior; if they attend the same school, middle-class children tend to provide educational benefits for children from lower-income households; middle-income households contribute

[6] Harvey, op. cit., p. 279.

more to central city revenues in the form of city income and property taxes than do lower-income households; and, most importantly, the middle-income household in the central city occupies a residential location which would otherwise be occupied by other low-income households. Relocation of middle-income groups to the suburbs, therefore, results in a massive welfare loss for the original low-income residents of the central city.

Once interterritorial bargaining is introduced, however, it becomes possible to offer those whose relocation would impose negative externalities some compensation to stay. This might take the form of provision of services for which the demand of relocatees is high, e.g., cultural facilities. Bargaining and compensation of this nature would permit a solution which is superior (in terms of maximizing individual utilities and resultant social welfare) to that offered by the game of conflict in which strategies are relocational.

In brief, there are good reasons for believing that a *de facto territorial organization* resulting from private coordination by relocation strategies does not eliminate the necessity for bargaining to maximize social welfare. Bargaining is required both between locators in the same territory and between locators in different territories. This brings us to the topic of the public coordination of allocative decisions.

PUBLIC COORDINATION

The difficulties posed by bargaining have already been reviewed. They include the disincentives to bargain and the inefficiency of bargaining with increasing numbers. Consideration of these difficulties would suggest that, in order to meet a demand for some coordination of individual resource allocations and to meet it in as efficient a manner as possible, some form of coercive organization constraining the property rights of individuals is desirable. This demand is met by a centralized, collective decision-making process; and this process is empowered by a constitution to provide coordination by means of universally binding decisions.

In other words, new, higher-level decision-making units are established as a result of the coordination needs created by the allocative decisions of lower-level decision-making units such as individual households. The higher-level decision-making units obviously are interpretable as governments. Like the lower-level decision-making units, governments must allocate resources to various productive ends in exchange for which they will receive the continued support of those lower-level units who put them in office. The products in question are known to economists as "public goods."

The definition of public good employed here is that commonly used by economists:

> "Goods which are consumed by all those who are members of a given community, country, or geographical area in such a manner that consumption or use by one member does not detract from consumption or use by another."[7]

The public good has two traits which distinguish it from the private good:

---

[7] Albert O. Hirschman, *Exit, Voice and Loyalty*, Cambridge, Mass.: Harvard University Press, 1970, p. 101.

(1) nonexclusion and (2) equal availability. None of those "who are members of a given community, country, or geographical area" can be excluded from the benefits provided by a public good. Nobody within a municipality, therefore, can be excluded from receiving the benefits of protection by the municipal fire service.

Equal availability signifies that consumption by one individual does not detract from consumption of the public good in question by another individual. Theoretically, one citizen's consumption of the city's garbage collection service does not affect either negatively or positively another citizen's consumption of that good.

Public goods produced by governments clearly fulfill a coordinative role. Some public goods take the form of legislation to limit some of the grosser negative externalities to which citizens are subjected—air pollution is a case in point. The geographic nature of this coordinative activity is made explicit in such institutional forms as land use zoning. The constraint on property rights implied by coordination is also apparent. In zoning, for example, the aim is to minimize the negative externalities resulting from the proximity of incompatible land users to one another. Housing codes attempt to eliminate the negative externalities created for residential property owners by inadequate property maintenance by neighbors.

Other public goods take the form of services which would be consumed, if purchase was purely private, at a socially suboptimal level. Public health and education services are instances of this; in both cases individuals would privately allocate resources only to the point at which their own utilities would be satisfied. Such allocative decisions would not take into account the important externalities accruing to the rest of society in the form of, say, a reduced level of contagious disease or a well-informed, civically-inclined population.

Like private goods, public goods provided by governments are purchased at a price: the tax collected from the individual. Unlike the case of private goods, however, the individual cannot consume a chosen quantity of a public good at a particular *unit* price. Pure public goods are available equally to all so that all must consume the same amount.

It is important to note that the concept of the public good is in many ways an abstraction from reality. Most public goods have some private aspect to them in terms of restricted availability or exclusion. Such public goods are referred to as "impure public goods." Although no one in a municipality can be excluded from the use of a municipal fire service, there may be variations in availability depending on distance from the fire station. Moreover there may be exclusion rules for the consumption of public goods: the income criterion employed in the allocation of public housing exemplifies this. We will find that in many ways impure public goods are more interesting to the geographer than the pure variety.

The Spatial Product of Public Coordination. The spatial product of public coordination of individual allocative decisions is a de jure territorial organization consisting of a set of discrete bounded spaces. *Each such space is occupied by those lower-level decision-making units whose* *allocative decisions are coordinated by the same collective decision-making process.*

Commonly such spaces are known as "jurisdictions." They have two properties which underline the forces generating them: compactness and boundedness. Compactness derives from the locational closeness of the individual decision-making units constituting a jurisdiction; this locational closeness in turn stems from the spatial correlates of the externalities produced by the allocative activities which are to be publicly controlled.

Jurisdictional boundedness, on the other hand, derives ultimately from the nature of public coordination. Public coordination modifies property rights. All resource allocation involves the use of an absolutely immobile resource—land, subdivided into unambiguously defined parcels. A spatial aggregation of parcels, such as that implied by a jurisdiction, has an outer boundary. Any public constraint on the use of such property, therefore, applies within the outer boundary of the properties owned by the individuals demanding public coordination. The result is a jurisdictional boundary which is clearly defined and absolute.

The Welfare Implications of Public Coordination. Public coordination within the context of a set of jurisdictions does not eliminate disutilities. Further, given the externality nature of these disutilities, public coordination does not completely eliminate the problem of locational conflict. Two types of locational conflict are generated: those *between* jurisdictions and those *within* jurisdictions between superordinate authorities and subordinate decision-making units. The latter would include conflicts ensuing from the negative externalities imposed by a government on some subset of its constituent decision-making units.

Between Jurisdictions: Governments may be viewed much as individuals are viewed as participants in a private economy; i.e., as resource allocators who attempt to maximize their utility. Assuming a democratic system, maximization of government utility is dependent upon maximization of the social welfare of the population to which the government is accountable. Governmental allocation, however, may have implications for the utilities and disutilities experienced by populations in other jurisdictions. In interjurisdictional relationships, therefore, as in the relationships between lower-level decision-making units, one can anticipate externality effects and locational conflict.

One of the clearest cases of this results from the exclusionary zoning policies of suburban municipalities. These policies are apparent in many of the nation's metropolitan areas. In these areas, much suburban land is zoned for residential populations occupying large lots. The motivation behind this zoning policy is that large lots will be so expensive as to restrict property development to upper-income groups. These groups will prefer a relatively expensive home to be constructed on the lot; in addition, residential densities will be limited. Consequently, the assessed property value per capita will be maximized. This permits the suburb the luxury of relatively large expenditures in such functional areas as education along with a low property tax rate.

This utility-maximizing allocative behavior, however, imposes indirect costs on central-city jurisdictions. In particular it restricts the residential choice of the low-income populations of central cities and imposes a continuing fiscal burden on the central city: relatively large demands for poverty-linked services must be met from a property tax revenue that declines as single-occupancy, middle-income homes are converted to multiple occupancy, lower-class use; as apartment buildings are abandoned under the impact of higher tax rates; and as business relocates to suburban jurisdictions. A consequence is the contemporary conflict between suburb and central city.

Like lower-level decision-making units, governments have a range of private coordinating strategies which they may engage in. Some of these are analogues of the relocation-option of the individual household. While relocation itself is clearly not an option, governments can and do pursue policies which affect the relocational decisions of individual households. The central-city government, for example, may attempt to attract middle-class residents back into the central city; this might be achieved by the construction of luxury housing under the auspices of urban renewal programs. The retention of middle-class populations can also be facilitated by a variety of policies: properties in middle-class neighborhoods may be under-assessed for property tax purposes.

Other government policies represent forms of private bargaining. The central city may negotiate with suburban municipalities for a subsidy toward the provision of those central-city services from which the whole metropolitan area benefits: a zoo, an art gallery, a city library, etc.

For reasons similar to those outlined for lower-level decision-making units, policies affecting household location rather than private bargaining tend to be favored. Consequently, the sum of social welfare across all localized populations is not maximized. The need for some coercive, collective decision-making process at the higher level which places limits on the property rights of governments again becomes evident. A tangible expression of this need consists of demands for metropolitan integration and the replacement of the jurisdictionally fragmented metropolis by a single unified metro-government.

Within Jurisdictions: The second type of locational conflict derives from externalities imposed by superordinate authorities on subordinates; in particular, governments impose negative externalities on some of their constituent decision-making units. This is true whether the superordinate authority is a municipality regulating the activities of households and firms or a council of metropolitan governments coordinating the activities of individual municipalities. These conflicts may derive from either heterogeneity in demands for coordination or from the impurity of the public good being provided.

It is rare that tastes within a jurisdiction are homogeneous. Rather, a government is more likely to confront an electorate across which there are differences in demand for a variety of public goods. As discussed earlier, however, public goods are supplied in a given quantity at a given price. The taxpayer, for example, may have to consume more education than he would, given a free choice. In this case the locational conflict is between the individual and that majority in the jurisdiction imposing a negative externality on him via representative government.

Other locational conflicts can be traced to the variations in availability characteristic of impure public goods. The quality of schooling may vary from one neighborhood school to another within the same jurisdiction. In a context of homogeneous demand curves, this may result in a welfare loss in underprovided neighborhoods and demands for increased provision.

Private locational strategies are easy to imagine in the context of these locational conflicts. The individual household, for instance, may move into a jurisdiction where policy outputs more closely match its tastes.[8] In other contexts, the household may relocate away from the neighborhood in which provision of education is suboptimal into neighborhoods in which it is more nearly optimal.

Private bargaining is also feasible. The strategic bargaining of the industrial firm when confronted by demands for pollution control is a case in point. Important bargaining resources for the firm include its control of employment and its ability to threaten unemployment if pollution control measures are pressed.

As with responses to households imposing externalities on other households, relocation or private bargaining is hardly likely to provide optimal levels of the externalities in question. Coordination by means of *collectivization of property rights* once again becomes necessary. The participants in locational conflicts within jurisdictions in the metropolitan area, therefore, are rarely individual citizens. Rather they are groups of citizens organized collectively and who have voluntarily donated control of some of their resources, such as their time, in order to obtain a public good in the form of redress of some localized problem. Local residents' associations, neighborhood organizations and local shopkeepers' associations therefore are the more important vehicles by which collective resolution of locational conflict is sought.

The tools of analysis which we use in understanding locational conflicts of the type discussed in this section were employed also in previous sections of this chapter. This suggests that it might be possible to define a relatively simple model of locational conflict in an urban context. This is the task of the final section.

A Paradigm of Locational Conflict and Conflict Resolution

Initially, one can assume decision-making units at any number of geographical scales. On a micro-scale they might be households and firms; on a macro-scale they could be jurisdictions. Each decision-making unit has a number of resources which are allocated to activities which maximize its utility. Allocation is governed by a set of property rights specifying the uses to which the different resources can be put. From these private allocations, externalities can be anticipated which create localized stress and locational conflict. The conflict is locational in the sense that it results from a conflict between the utility-maximizing goals

---

[8] For an exposition of this viewpoint see Charles Tiebout, "A Pure Theory of Local Expenditures," *Journal of Political Economy*, vol. 64, 1956, pp. 416-424.

of the individual decision-making units and the allocative behavior of other decision-making units located in the vicinity. The conflict may be between decision-making units at the same geographical scale (e.g., between households *or* between municipalities) or, it may be between decision-making units at different geographical scales (e.g., between a household and the municipality in which it is located).

Locational conflicts can be resolved by either private locational strategies or by private bargaining. The individual household may move just as the individual jurisdiction can affect that movement. A variety of intermunicipal or interhousehold bargaining procedures can also be envisaged.

As we have been at pains to point out, private solutions are suboptimal. Externalities will remain in the form of residual localized stress. Further coordination by collective control of some of the individual decision-making units' property rights could make at least one unit better off without making any other one worse off. At the micro-level, therefore, individual households cede some sovereignty over the use of their property to a superordinate authority; coordination is then achieved by a modification of the property rights of individual households. At the macro-level, individual jurisdictions grant some of their sovereignty over the property rights of their constituent decision-making units to a superordinate jurisdiction such as a council of metropolitan governments.

The collectivization of property rights and the vesting of them in a superordinate authority, therefore, creates new decision-making units on a new and larger geographical scale. These units in turn create externalities for other units at the same geographic scale or at smaller geographic scales and a new cycle of locational conflict and conflict resolution is generated.

The Organization of the Book

In the remainder of this book the conceptual model outlined and exemplified in this chapter is applied to an examination of conflicts between localities within metropolitan areas.

The next chapter attempts to define and explain the territorial organization of metropolitan areas. The components of that organization —populations localized in jurisdictions and neighborhoods—provide the entities between which locational conflict occurs and which are so prominent in the resolution of that conflict. At the same time territorial organization itself provides important evidence on the nature of conflict resolution in an urban context.

Chapter 3 examines conflict between the components of the de jure territorial organization of the metropolitan area. Conflicts between the central city municipality and surrounding suburban municipalities in a metropolitan area are discussed here. Conflict, however, also occurs between populations localized in neighborhoods within jurisdictions. Intrajurisdictional conflicts, therefore, are discussed in Chapter 4.

Finally, given this backdrop of data and interpretation, Chapter 5 examines the locational manifestations of urban conflicts from a prescriptive point of view. In brief, what are the geographic merits and demerits of alternative policy approaches to the urban crisis?

CHAPTER 2

THE TERRITORIAL ORGANIZATION OF METROPOLITAN AREAS

Two of the more dominant features of the spatial organization of metropolitan areas in the United States are *jurisdictional fragmentation* corresponding to the de jure territorial organization discussed in Chapter 1 and, within jurisdictions, *residential segregation by income, ethnicity, and race into a set of discrete neighborhoods*—the de facto territorial organization of the city. Both of these features represent the outcome of conflict resolution processes at the level of the individual household. Both provide the context for an understanding of contemporary conflicts within the metropolitan area between individuals and jurisdictions, and also between jurisdictions.

The aims of this chapter are twofold: first, to describe and explain the features of metropolitan territorial organization and, second, to sketch their role in the metropolitan political system. Initially, we discuss de facto territorial organization, de jure territorial organization is then considered, and, last, their interrelationships are examined.

De Facto Territorial Organization

The social geography of the cities of North America shows a high degree of residential segregation based not only on the race criterion but also on such variables as social class or ethnic origin. In some cities, religion is the important criterion with, for example, clearly demarcated Jewish or Roman Catholic areas; in the city of Belfast, Northern Ireland, residential segregation by religion is the major feature of the city's social map.[1] In other cities, the regional origin of immigrants may provide a basis for some residential segregation; in a number of cities in Ohio, for example, distinct areas of lower-class housing are dominated by poor whites from

---

[1] Emrys Jones, *Social Geography of Belfast,* New York: Oxford University Press, 1960.

West Virginia or Kentucky. In a sense, therefore, we can conceive of the city as being organized into a set of neighborhoods or territories, the inhabitants of each neighborhood exhibiting greater similarity to one another than to the residents of other neighborhoods.

The spatial organization of the city into a set of discrete territories or neighborhoods homogeneous with respect to race and/or social class can be explained in terms of demand and supply considerations. The demand for the socially or racially homogeneous territory derives largely from: (1) the demand for accessibility to those regarded as providing positive externalities and (2) the demand for physical distance from those regarded as providing negative externalities. The externalities at issue can be identified as "public behavior externalities" and "status externalities" respectively. They are highly correlated with social class and race.

Important forms of public behavior concern: (a) levels of property maintenance—most prefer that neighbors maintain their property to a degree which enhances their own residential properties; (b) crime—a negative externality for all those affected; (c) general public comportment including quiet, sobriety, and tidiness; and (d) child behavior—most parents prefer that the peer group contacts which their children enjoy in school and in play should reinforce the values inculcated in the home.

While preferences for these forms of public behavior are fairly homogeneous from one social class to another, the ability to provide them is distributed more unequally. Budgetary constraints prevent lower-class achievement of property maintenance levels which are satisfactory by middle-class standards. Class-specific socialization produces a cultural divergence between middle-class and lower-class children so that lower-class children are unlikely to be able to reinforce the cultural values instilled in the middle-class child. The reduced sanctions on petty crime characteristic of the lower class also reduce their acceptability as neighbors for middle-class residents.

This is not to say, however, that the forms of public behavior preferred by lower-income groups are exactly the same as those preferred by middle- and upper-income groups. There is evidence that some preferred public behaviors are lower-class – specific. These include a preference for provision of social security on a highly informal basis. Lower-class communities are noted for the range of informal welfare services which they provide for their members. In a survey of lower-class black neighborhoods in Detroit, it was found that out of the 463 separate contacts reported by the respondents, 224 were of a helping nature.[2] Though no comparative data exist on the extent and type of mutual aid relationships existing within a middle-class area, it would almost certainly be revealing in its contrast.

The differentiation of ability to provide certain externalities by social class and to a lesser degree differentiation of preferences by the same criterion has implications for residential segregation by race. To the extent that black populations compared with white populations are overwhelm-

---

[2] Eleanor P. Wolf and Charles N. Lebeaux, *Change and Renewal in an Urban Community*, New York: Praeger, 1969, pp. 201-202.

ingly lower-class, one should expect some residential segregation by race. Nevertheless, the observed magnitude of residential segregation by race when holding the effects of social class constant suggests that other externalities are at issue.

Some of these may be "status externalities." A household residing in a neighborhood occupied largely by those of high status gains status from such residence when all other determinants of status are taken into account. Status is evaluated in both social and ethnic terms and status externalities probably account for a large proportion of existing residential segregation by race. Racial transition, for example, almost invariably provokes statements as to how the neighborhood has "gone downhill."

Much concern over the negative externalities imposed by undesirable social and racial groups occurs in the form of a concern over *property values*. This is well known in the case of white fears of black invasion. Similar concerns are also expressed by middle-class households vis-à-vis lower-class households. While the pricing stratification of the housing market tends to sharply limit the possibility of lower-class purchase of homes in middle-class neighborhoods, some isolated case studies have revealed the importance of the property value consideration. A case in point is provided by middle-class reactions to the establishment of a lower-class housing estate in Oxford, England during the 1930s. The conflict took tangible expression in the form of a wall built across a connecting highway by individuals from the middle-class community in order to restrict movement between the two neighborhoods.[3] In the ensuing legal conflict over the removal of the walls—called the Cutteslowe Walls—widespread concern over property values was revealed among middle-class householders. Prior to the removal of the wall in the late 1950s, 81 percent of a sample from the middle-class neighborhood felt that the removal of the wall would lower their property values. Interestingly enough only 23 percent of the sample from the lower-class estate felt that removal would lower property values in that same middle-class neighborhood.

The conclusion to be drawn from these externality considerations is that, in residential site selection, households demand not only housing but also neighborhoods. These are evaluated in terms of the positive externalities which their residents provide. In some way, therefore, the housing market must be organized to supply neighborhoods which will: (1) attract and continue to attract a group of residents supplying a particular range of positive externalities and (2) exclude those who, though they may prefer the same positive externalities, are unable to provide them.

The first constraint is relatively easy to satisfy. It could be achieved, for example, by a process of neighborhood growth in which individuals exchange housing in order to maximize accessibility to those providing the positive externalities preferred. The second constraint is more difficult to satisfy. In the American city, the major problems are the exclusion of low-income groups from middle-income neighborhoods and the exclusion

[3] Peter Collison, *The Cutteslowe Walls,* London: Faber and Faber, 1963.

of blacks from white neighborhoods. The preferences of lower-class households for neighborhoods which are socially mixed are much stronger than those of middle-class households. The preferences of blacks for racially integrated neighborhoods are much stronger than those of whites for such neighborhoods.

For example, in a sample of black respondents drawn from fifteen major U.S. cities, only one black respondent out of eight favored residential separation by race. The vast majority preferred "integration" either in the positive sense of "racial balance" or in the nondiscriminatory sense of race being irrelevant to decisions about neighborhood.[4] White preferences for racially integrated neighborhoods are much more modest with only about 50 percent expressing such preference.

The housing market, therefore, is consciously structured to meet a demand for neighborhoods from which those of lower income and the black can be excluded. Two mechanisms currently are operative: (1) the construction of homes in large developments homogeneous with respect to housing price; by setting the price sufficiently high, lower-income groups can be excluded on the basis of their budgetary constraints, and (2) the development of a dual housing market in which real estate brokers and mortgagors structure the supply of housing in a racially discriminatory manner. Despite federal legislation to the contrary, it is quite apparent that the real estate industry continues to guide blacks into either black or "changing" neighborhoods while keeping them out of white neighborhoods by a variety of more or less implausible ploys. Again, despite their lack of legal force, a number of neighborhoods maintain associations which must approve clients before neighborhood houses are sold.

The continuing legal challenge to the dual housing market and the difficulties of controlling a variety of externalities simply by means of the socially or racially homogeneous neighborhood lead to a search for a more effective territorial organization. This takes the form of a de jure territorial organization.

De Jure Territorial Organization

Despite variations between metropolitan areas, it is possible to think in terms of a general model of de jure territorial organization applicable to most metropolitan areas in the United States. Generally, two facets of that organization are apparent: jurisdictional fragmentation and the presence of a large central-city municipality surrounded by smaller suburban municipalities.

Metropolitan areas are subdivided into a multiplicity of municipalities, school districts, nonschool special districts and counties, each with its own powers to provide services and raise revenues. The average number of local government units per metropolitan area is eighty-seven. Clearly, however, larger metropolitan areas have more local government units and, in some cases, this number reaches almost astronomical proportions; for example,

---

[4] Angus Campbell and Howard Schuman, "Racial Attitudes in Fifteen American Cities," in *Supplemental Studies for the National Advisory Commission on Civil Disorders,* Washington, D.C.: U.S. Government Printing Office, 1968, p. 16.

the Chicago metropolitan area has over 1,000 local government units.

Most central-city municipalities in metropolitan areas find themselves hemmed in by a ring of independent suburbs. These cut off the central cities from unincorporated suburban land and, therefore, eliminate the possibility of expansion by annexation.

Little attention has been given to the social homogeneity or heterogeneity of municipalities within a metropolitan area. Intuitively, it seems reasonable to suggest that the central city is much more diversified in both social class and in racial terms than most suburban municipalities. The latter tend to be specialized—there are middle-class suburbs and some blue-collar suburbs. In addition, there are some suburbs given over largely to industrial and to commercial land uses with only small residential populations. There are, however, very few black suburban municipalities.

Within a demand-supply framework, demands are for accessibility to those providing positive externalities and exclusion of those providing negative externalities. Many positive externalities cannot be provided and many negative externalities cannot be excluded by the socially and/or racially homogeneous neighborhood. Local tax resources, for example, cannot be applied merely to the satisfaction of neighborhood needs. Within jurisdictions, the fiscal system works to redistribute income to some degree by using taxes from wealthy neighborhoods to subsidize public services in poorer neighborhoods. Also, there is no certainty that the local school system will continue to have a largely white middle-class student body. Government-ordered busing within school systems may destroy this product of the neighborhood school principle. In brief, residential segregation does not assure control of a variety of externalities which affect environmental quality.

Provision of such positive externalities depends upon a *respecification of property rights*. In this respecification, each member of the nascent jurisdiction cedes control of some of his property rights to the local community. Maximally effective coordination requires coercion and coercion requires some cession of rights over the use of resources. At the same time, however, the nascent political community (e.g., municipality) obtains rights which the larger community (e.g., county) has held regarding the use of property by individuals within the smaller community—for example, rights to zone land for specific purposes or rights to tax property. The area within which property rights have been respecified is then known as a jurisdiction.

Casual empiricism suggests that this interpretation of jurisdiction formation has a good deal of merit. Much suburban incorporation is and has been of the defensive variety. Where annexation by the central city has seemed imminent, incorporation has provided a means of thwarting city control of local land-use and fiscal policy.

The supply of local jurisdictional autonomy is constrained by the rights which the citizen has to: (1) withdraw controls over the use of his property which are currently held by other jurisdictions and (2) transfer those same controls to a new local jurisdiction. In the American suburban context, this specifically involves the right to incorporate as a municipality. This is a function of state law and the encouragement which it gives to suburban incorporation relative to the annexation of unincorporated land by existing municipalities.

Prior to 1900, annexation was relatively easy and accounts for the large areas covered by most of today's central cities. Since then areal growth of central cities has slowed down appreciably and most of the growth of metropolitan areas has been associated with the incorporation of new independent municipalities. Much of the responsibility for this locational pattern devolves to a state legislative context; after 1900, this context favored the incorporation of new suburban municipalities rather than annexation. By a variety of devices, state legislatures, increasingly dominated by a coalition of legislators from rural and suburban areas, attempted to reduce the possibility of annexation of their constituencies by central cities. Power in annexation procedures, therefore, was often shifted away from the central city toward the suburban area. At the same time as annexation was made more difficult for central cities, the legal procedures for municipal incorporation remained extremely favorable to small unincorporated suburban communities. In particular, they continued to allow very small communities—often less than 500 in population—to incorporate and establish municipal governments. The result was the locational pattern of the central city with its surrounding independent suburbs which we see today.

More recently, there have been efforts to change the legal context in favor of central cities, though in many cases this has been too late since central cities are already surrounded and cut off from unincorporated territory by their suburban ring. A number of states, including Ohio, Georgia, Arizona and North Carolina, have passed "anti-incorporation" laws. These laws contain the idea of creating around a municipality a belt of land in which new incorporations cannot take place unless the existing municipality agrees to the incorporation or refuses to annex an area when asked to do so. In Arizona, for example, the belt is three miles in width around municipalities of less than 5,000 and six miles in width for larger towns and cities. No new incorporation can take place in these belts unless the existing municipality agrees or refuses to annex when petitioned.

This jurisdictional fragmentation would be of limited significance for locational conflict within the metropolitan area if it were not for the powers which the resultant authorities have. Some idea of their responsibilities can be gained from Table 2.1 which lists the proportion of local funds constituting state-local expenditures on selected urban services for 1966 to 1967. Fiscally, local governments are particularly responsible for such services as public safety, sanitation, water supply, parks, and recreation; they enjoy diminished responsibility in the areas of welfare and education. Nevertheless, as the second column of the table shows, in absolute terms the amount of money which local governments must raise for educational purposes is especially onerous.

What type of local government is fiscally responsible for a given service varies from one metropolitan area to another and sometimes from state to state. For example, in the cities of New York, Boston and Baltimore, the municipality provides educational services; in Philadelphia, St. Louis, San Francisco, Denver and New Orleans, on the other hand, school districts are independent of the municipality. Likewise, sanitation and water are sometimes provided by municipalities and, at other times, by special districts charged with this responsibility.

Variations in the state assignment of responsibility for funding welfare are particularly critical and Table 2.1 is misleading in this regard. In some states, the state assumes complete responsibility and in others, such as New York and Ohio, the individual county is charged with this responsibility.

Funding of most local government expenditures is primarily through the property tax. This is true for public education, police and fire, highway maintenance, local parks and recreation, public health, welfare, and housing programs. Services such as water and sanitation, on the other hand, are financed largely through user charges. The property tax is a flat-rate tax applied to the assessed value of private property; public

Table 2.1. Financing of Selected Urban Services, 1966-67 (dollar amounts in billions).

Selected urban services	Amount spent by Governments actually providing the service			How state-local spending is financed (percent)*		
	State	Local	Com-bined	Federal funds	State funds	Local funds
Income-redistribution activities:						
Welfare	$4.3	$4.0	$ 8.2	51%	35%	14%
Health & hospitals	3.4	3.3	6.6	6	48	46
Housing programs	—†	1.5	1.5	47	6	47
Public schools	0.3	27.8	28.1	7	38	55
Resource-allocation activities:						
Police, correction & fire	1.2	4.5	5.7	—	21	79
Transportation (except highways)	1.3	2.1	2.4	4	12	84
Water supply & water treatment	—‡	4.3	4.3	2	2	96
Local parks & recreation	—‡	1.3	1.3	3	4	93
Sanitation (except sewerage)	—	0.9	0.9	—	—	100
Libraries	—†	0.5	0.5	10	10	80
TOTAL, selected services	$ 9.4	$50.1	$59.5	13%	31%	56%

* These columns describe the source of funds for the state-local direct expenditure shown in the preceding columns. The federal government also makes the direct expenditure for federal programs, for example, for the air traffic control system. The federal funds shown in this table include only federal aid to state and local government.

† Less than $50 million.

‡ There is some direct state government expenditure for urban water supply and for urban parks, but it is small and difficult to separate out from published data.

Source: Dick Netzer, *Economics and Urban Problems*, New York: Basic Books, 1970, p. 172.

property such as schools, federal and state buildings are exempt. An important feature of the property tax, however, is its regressive character. Because the taxation rate is a flat rate applied to the assessed value of property, these taxes represent a higher proportion of income for lower-income property owners or renters than for high-income groups. This is demonstrated rather clearly in Table 2.2.

Table 2.2. Estimates of Housing Property Taxes as a Percentage of Income, by Income Class.

	United States, 1959	
Income class	Single-Family Homeowners (percent)	Renters (percent)
Less than $2,000	6.4	8.5
$ 2,000 − 3,000	4.5	3.9
3,000 − 4,000	3.7	3.0
4,000 − 5,000	3.3	2.5
5,000 − 7,000	3.1	2.1
7,000−10,000	2.8	1.8
10,000−15,000	2.6	1.6
Over $15,000	2.3	1.4

Source: Dick Netzer, *Economics of the Property Tax*, Washington, D.C.: Brookings Institution, 1966, Table 3.8.

A final consideration of the fragmentation of local authority relates to the allocation of responsibility for zoning of land use. This is a highly important function of municipalities in controlling the movement of different types of land users. Since zoning power is largely vested in municipalities and counties, the act of incorporation assumes an especially critical significance for communities wishing to manipulate their local land-use environment.

In contradistinction to the socially or racially homogeneous neighborhood which constitutes the individual element of a de facto territorial organization, the jurisdiction enjoys some control of individual property rights. In some respects, however, this dichotomy is somewhat unfair to the reality of the situation. In addition, both the de facto and the de jure territorial organization appear to be linked in a hierarchical manner. The interrelationships of the two types of territorial organization are discussed next.

Territorial Organization of Metropolitan Areas: An Integrated View

Implicit in the discussion of territorial organization so far has been a polarity. On the one hand, there is a territorial organization in which transfer of individual property rights to a central coordinating mechanism takes place. On the other hand, there is a de facto territorial organization in which there is no central coordinating mechanism and no transfer of property rights. Like many polarities this one seems to conceal the presence of a continuum.

Between these two polar types are those neighborhoods in which there is a central coordinating mechanism but in which the transfer of property rights is voluntary. Many neighborhoods, for example, have residents' associations designed to monitor any locational changes of significance to it and to organize neighborhood residents for lobbying purposes. Specifically, such organization is directed at the maintenance or enhancement of allocations which provide positive externalities in the neighborhood and at the exclusion of allocations which provide negative externalities. Effectiveness of such policies, however, depends upon the willingness of local residents to cede control over some of their resources to the neighborhood organization. Time must be made available by the residents for use by the organization. Individual residents may have to forego some of the discretionary power in the sale of property to outsiders; for example, in neighborhoods threatened by racial transition, residents planning to sell property are frequently asked to place it in the hands of an agency expressly established by a neighborhood association for the purpose of limiting the business carried on by block busters.[5] Clearly, the social and/or racial homogeneity of the neighborhood facilitates that homogeneity of preference which enables voluntary action to be forthcoming and to be sustained.

What is being defined, therefore, is a continuum of local political organization—at one end of the scale, the residentially segregated neighborhood which lacks any collective organization, through neighborhoods with some voluntary collective control, to jurisdictions with coercive collective control over the property rights of constituent households, firms, etc. at the other end of the scale.

The concept of a continuum is critical for an understanding of the operations of political systems and of the determination of which neighborhoods get what. Jurisdictional provision has a direct and indirect impact upon the environmental quality of the neighborhood. The locational pattern of jurisdictional provision, however, depends upon the supply of information from its constituent neighborhoods. The central coordinating mechanism of the jurisdiction requires information not only on what is required but what is not required. In addition, information is needed on the implications of a particular locational pattern of provision for the government's own utility. Thus, neighborhood organization is clearly important—it communicates wants and it can communicate threats. A reasonable prediction, therefore, would be that neighborhoods which are organized are more likely to enhance neighborhood quality than neighborhoods which are not.

Summary and Concluding Comments

In this chapter, the prevalent forms of territorial organization in American metropolitan areas have been discussed. De facto territorial organization takes the form of residential segregation into a set of discrete neighborhoods homogeneous with respect to income and race. These represent the outcome of demands for accessibility to those providing positive public

[5] Wolf and Lebeaux, op. cit., Chapter 3.

behavior and status externalities and for physical distance from those imposing negative externalities. In the selection of a residential location, therefore, households demand not only housing but also neighborhoods.

Supply is facilitated by the development of mechanisms excluding those imposing negative externalities and attracting those who will share their positive externalities with one another. These mechanisms include the offering of large-scale residential developments which are homogeneous with respect to price; homogeneous housing prices filter in those able to share their externalities while, by setting the price high enough, those who cannot supply the necessary externalities can be excluded. The second mechanism is that of the dual housing market in which the real estate industry and mortgagors allocate housing in a racially discriminatory manner.

Residential segregation into a set of neighborhoods, however, does not permit control of all the externalities bearing upon the environmental quality of the neighborhood. Many of these can only be handled by a coercive organization to which individual residents have yielded some of their property rights. Factors of demand similar to those generating a de facto territorial organization, therefore, also are important in producing a de jure territorial organization. Supply of local coercive control in this case has been facilitated by state law; since 1900, at least, this tended to favor suburban incorporation rather than annexation of the same land by central cities expanding at their edge. The end product has been jurisdictional fragmentation and constraints on the territorial expansion of the generally larger central-city jurisdiction.

The dichotomy between jurisdictions with their coercive control of individual property use, however, and residentially segregated neighborhoods lacking such a control mechanism is, in some respects, an oversimplification. In many neighborhoods, there is a control mechanism which takes the form of neighborhood organization designed to protect neighborhood interests; in such cases, however, the cession of property rights is purely voluntary.

One interpretation of which locations get what, therefore, would focus upon interneighborhood differences and the forces, such as neighborhood organization, which generate such differences. These issues are discussed in Chapter 4. A second interpretation, on the other hand, would focus upon interjurisdictional differences and the interjurisdictional relationships which produce them. This is discussed at length in the next chapter.

CHAPTER 3

METROPOLITAN FRAGMENTATION AND URBAN CONFLICT

The spatial organization of the metropolitan area into a set of jurisdictions, each having considerable latitude in funding and expenditure, generates a variety of conflicts. Given the existent fragmentation of authority to tax and spend, the expenditure capability of a jurisdiction will depend on the tax resources available within its boundaries. However, since demands for services are often inversely related to tax resources, needs may often go unmet in the area covered by one authority while elsewhere tax resources are far from fully exploited. This situation characterizes the relationships of central cities and independent suburbs in the United States and is known as the "central-city–suburban fiscal disparities problem." We will first examine the geography of this problem and then attempt to explain it.

Briefly, the central-city–suburban fiscal disparities problem refers to an imbalance between needs for government-provided public services and the tax resources with which to provide them. This has serious implications for the quality and quantity of public provision in both the central city and suburb. The service-needs/tax-capacity ratio tends to be particularly high in central cities and much lower in suburbs. Partly as a consequence of this, levels of service provision in such critical areas as education are often greater in the suburbs.

In the first section of this chapter, we take a general view of the fiscal disparities problem. We examine in greater detail the geography of demand for government-produced public services within metropolitan areas. We then discuss the tax resource geography of metropolitan areas and the implications of tax resource geography and the geography of demand for public services for spatial patterns of public provision. Next, we examine the applicability of the fiscal disparities problem to the highly critical area of education. And, last, we attempt to provide a quantitative picture of the geography of the disparity problem.

Fiscal Disparities: A General View

THE GEOGRAPHY OF DEMAND FOR PUBLIC SERVICES

Demand for public services tends to be much greater in central cities than in suburban areas. This is partly a result of the concentration there of poorer people, crime, and aging, often fire-prone housing.

Median incomes in central cities generally are appreciably lower than those prevailing in the surrounding suburban rings. These differences are

Table 3.1. City Shares of State Population and Public Assistance Recipients for Selected Cities, 1956 and 1966. *†*

City and Item	1956	1966	Percent Change 1956-1966
New York City			
Population	49.6%	44.2%	−10.9%
Total PA recipients	67.3	70.2	+ 4.3
AFDC recipients	74.0	71.7	− 3.1
Philadelphia			
Population	18.6	17.8	− 4.3
Total PA recipients	26.1	29.6	+ 13.4
AFDC recipients	29.4	32.8	+ 11.6
Baltimore			
Population	35.1	26.8	−23.6
Total PA recipients	64.3	66.4	+ 3.3
AFDC recipients	68.4	71.2	+ 4.1
Boston			
Population	17.2	13.6	−20.9
Total PA recipients	28.3	32.0	+ 13.1
AFDC recipients	36.4	38.4	+ 5.5
San Francisco			
Population	5.9	3.9	−33.9
Total PA recipients	5.4	4.9	− 9.3
AFDC recipients	5.0	4.6	− 8.0
St. Louis			
Population	19.4	15.5	−20.1
Total PA recipients	16.4	25.5	+ 55.5
AFDC recipients	24.6	37.1	+ 50.8

* Population data are for July 1955 and July 1965; recipient data are for June 1956 and June 1966.

† The cities listed tend to have much larger shares of their respective states' public assistance case-load than of their population. The dynamics of the problem are also interesting: a city's share of public assistance recipients generally changed relative to its share of the state's population in an adverse direction.

Source: Advisory Commission on Intergovernmental Relations, *Fiscal Balance in the American Federal System, Vol. 2: Metropolitan Fiscal Disparities,* Washington, D.C.: U.S. Government Printing Office, 1967, p. 41.

further underlined by statistics on unemployment. With only a few exceptions, rates of unemployment in 1960 were higher in central cities than in urban fringes. Generally, for every 1,000 central-city residents, 55 were unemployed while for urban fringes the comparable figure was 41. In some cases, the central-city–suburban difference was much larger. In Detroit, an astounding 9.9 percent of the central-city residents were unemployed compared with 5.9 percent in the suburbs. In the case of Newark, the comparable figures were 8.2 percent and 3.4 percent. Within central cities, unemployment rates reach particularly high levels in certain well-known slum areas.

Central-city poverty and unemployment are reflected in high demands for public assistance. These demands are apparent to some degree in data on the relative proportions of a given state's population and of its public assistance recipients respectively, located in central cities. In 1966, while New York City contained only 44.2 percent of the state's population, it contained 70.2 percent of all public assistance recipients in the state (refer to Table 3.1). In Baltimore, the disparity is even greater and in most cities the situation seems to be deteriorating further. In all of the cities for which data are presented, the respective city's share of state population has tended to grow at a slower rate than its share of state public assistance recipients.

While such central-city–suburban differences clearly impose a heavy burden on central cities there are other effects also which have repercussions on the demand for public services. The geography of poverty tends to be related to the geography of crime with consequent effects on the demand for more investment in local police forces. As Table 3.2 shows for robbery rates per 100,000 population in 1965, central cities are much more seriously affected than metropolitan areas as a whole.

Housing conditions also are importantly related to demands for public services. For example, inadequate housing creates fire and health hazards. Here again central-city populations are at a considerable disadvantage. Central-city housing is substantially older than that characteristically found in suburbs. In 1960, only 19.8 percent of the central-city homes

Table 3.2. Robbery Rates Per 100,000 Population for Selected Central Cities and Metropolitan Areas.

Area	Central City	Metropolitan Area
Chicago	420.8	244.3
Newark	379.8	109.4
Washington	358.8	153.2
Miami	241.2	164.2
Los Angeles	293.4	189.1
Cleveland	213.4	101.1
Houston	135.3	95.5
Dayton	129.6	55.2

Source: Advisory Commission on Intergovernmental Relations, *Fiscal Balance in the American Federal System, Vol. 2: Metropolitan Fiscal Disparities,* Washington, D.C.: U.S. Government Printing Office, 1967, p. 48.

had been built in the preceding decade; for suburban areas, the figure was 41.5 percent. In terms of the soundness of housing, the comparison also was unfavorable to central cities though not greatly so; in 1960, 20.4 percent of the central-city housing was declared to be unsound as compared with 15.6 percent of suburban housing. The unsound housing of the central city, however, tends to be overwhelmingly associated with the black ghetto.

THE GEOGRAPHY OF PUBLIC RESOURCES

Obviously, the unevenness in the distribution of demand for public services would pose no problem if there was a similar and proportional unevenness in the availability of the tax capacity from which to fund these services. In fact, tax capacity or the value of taxable resources is distributed quite perversely from the viewpoint of demand for services. Generally, tax capacity per capita is much higher in suburban locations. As a consequence, this has implications for the central-city government in meeting the demands made upon it for public provision.

Compared to the suburbs, the property tax bases of central cities show a long term decline; in some cases, the decline is absolute rather than relative. This is largely associated with the movement of businesses and middle-class homeowners from the central city to the suburbs. Businesses provide an important source of property tax revenue. Their increasing suburbanization since 1945 has posed serious revenue problems for central cities. This overall shift is summarized by figures on retail sales and on industrial employment. While in central cities, retail sales in 1963 were only 4.8 percent above their level in 1958—hardly enough to offset the effects of price inflation—suburban retail activity registered an increase in sales of over 45 percent over the same period of time. In manufacturing, central-city employment in 1963 was 6 percent less than what it has been five years earlier; suburban employment in manufacturing was over 15 percent greater.

Consequently, central cities have had and are having to make greatly increased tax efforts. These increased tax efforts are reflected not only in increased property taxes but also in the introduction of local nonproperty taxes. Local taxes in the central cities of the thirty-seven largest Standard Metropolitan Statistical Areas (SMSAs) in 1965 amounted to 7.6 percent of the personal income of residents as compared with 5.6 percent outside the central cities. Further, these averages concealed some very high taxes in individual cities. In Newark, the central-city–suburban disparity in per capita taxes as a percent of per capita income was a very high 6.8 percentage points; in the central city, taxes amounted to 13.3 percent of personal income as compared with 6.5 percent in the suburban ring. In Washington, D.C. the comparable figures were 9.7 percent and 4.2 percent.

THE GEOGRAPHY OF PUBLIC PROVISION

The relatively unfavorable service demand/tax capacity ratio of central cities compared to their suburbs is mirrored in the quality and quantity of public services produced. This is most apparent in the area of educational expenditures. Although, in 1957, educational expenditures per pupil were slightly higher in the central cities of the thirty-seven largest SMSAs, in 1965, the advantage had clearly been transferred to suburban areas which spent $1.27 for every dollar spent by central cities.

At the same time, central cities had to spend much more on public safety and sanitation services than their suburban neighbors. This partly explains the disparity in educational provision. In 1965, the central cities of the thirty-seven largest SMSAs spent one hundred dollars more per capita on noneducational expenditures than did the suburbs. In general, therefore, central cities spend a much smaller proportion of their total revenue on education than do suburbs. This is the problem of "municipal overburden."

In dynamic terms, the fiscal disparities problem appears to worsen. Relatively, the central cities are falling further behind suburban municipalities in their tax bases and in public provision. Only in demand do central cities have an unfortunate advantage in terms of growth.

Table 3.3 describes the problem in a nutshell in terms of per capita gaps between central city and suburb in the period from 1957 to 1965. In 1957, while central-city tax revenue per capita was $38 less than in the suburbs, in 1965, it was $48 less—and this despite the much greater tax efforts made by central cities. This is a clear indication of the way in

Table 3.3. Changes in Central-City–Suburb Per Capita Expenditure and Revenue Gaps, 1957-65.

Item	Education Expenditure	Noneducation Expenditure	Tax Revenue
Per capita gap			
1957	−$25	+$ 69	−$38
1965	− 47	+ 100	− 48

Source: Advisory Commission on Intergovernmental Relations, *Fiscal Balance in the American Federal System, Vol. 2: Metropolitan Fiscal Disparities,* Washington, D.C.: U.S. Government Printing Office, 1967, p. 87.

which the redistribution of business and middle-class residents has brought benefits to the suburbs at the expense of the central city. The problem of municipal overburden also seems to be increasing. While the expenditure gap has moved in favor of the city in noneducational expenditure, quite the reverse has occurred in educational expenditure. Indeed, the fiscal disparities problem both in its static and in its dynamic aspects is nowhere more graphically illustrated than in the area of education. It is to that that we now turn.

Fiscal Disparities: The Case of Education

THE GEOGRAPHY OF DEMAND FOR EDUCATION

While it might appear at first glance that the geographical distribution of pupils between central city and suburbs is an adequate characterization of the geography of demand for education in metropolitan areas, such is not the case for at least four reasons. First, and most importantly, the typically poorer and often black student of the central-city school system requires a much greater investment of educational resources in order to bring him up to the achievement levels more characteristic of the suburban student with his typically richer background. Investments in education include not only those made by the formal school system itself but also by the student's parents. For example, primitive attempts to measure educational capital invested in a child in the preschool period suggest that these disparities are very large. Assuming that a more educated mother has a greater educational effect on her child per unit time spent than a less educated mother and computing the value of that investment as equivalent to the amount of money the parent could make by spending the same time in employment we find that, for example: a child whose mother did not graduate from the 8th grade will have about $4,000 of educational capital invested in him while a child whose mother graduated from college will have about $16,000 to $17,000 invested in him.[1]

The same line of argument can be extended to explain the poorer child's inability to sustain high levels of achievement when exposed to the same intensity of formal educational investment as a child from a richer background. The child from the poorer home does not have the same informal educational experiences. Presumably, neighborhood differences are also critical for such informal educational experiences.

A second factor increasing the demand for per pupil investment in education in central-city locations relates to certain disadvantageous features of the cost structure of education there. As a case in point, land costs are considerably higher in central-city locations; Detroit, for example, paid over $100,000 per acre for school sites purchased in 1967 while in surrounding suburban districts the price was about $6,000.

It is in the cost of teaching staff, however, that the adverse cost structure of the central city becomes most apparent. Teachers frequently demand an increment in pay as inducement to work in central-city schools over and above that which they will accept in suburban school districts. Also working to raise the cost of teachers in central-city school systems is their age. Charles Benson has pointed out that for a number of reasons central-city school systems tend to have staffs characterized by considerable seniority.[2] Since teachers are paid largely on the basis of seniority, it follows that central-city school systems often will pay more per staff member than suburban districts in which staff seniority is not so apparent.

The final cost consideration is that of security. Vandalism tends to be a much greater problem in central-city districts. This is reflected not only in the cost of replacing vandalized facilities but also in the increased cost of insurance.

A third major factor inflating the demand for investment in education in central cities is the increasing age and obsolescence of the physical

[1] *Hearings Before the Select Committee on Equal Educational Opportunity of the U.S. Senate, 91st Congress: 2nd Session on Equal Educational Opportunity, Part 7—Inequality of Economic Resources,* 1970, p. 3443.
[2] Charles E. Benson, *Education Finance and Its Relation to School Opportunities of Minority Groups.* Background Study for U.S. Commission on Civil Rights, 1966 (unpublished).

capital employed. In the Northeast, 43 percent of the central-city elementary schools are over forty years old while in the suburbs only 18 percent are over forty years old. This is clearly a problem which is more important in the older urbanized sections of the nation such as the Northeast and the Midwest; in Los Angeles, for instance, only 9 percent of the elementary schools are over forty-five years old. Nevertheless, within the older urbanized sections of the nation, the need to rebuild does pose a potential drain on resources and one which must be met if a more adequate environment for learning is to be provided.

Fourth, and finally, public school enrollments are being inflated by the closing of central-city parochial schools and the shift of a large number of their pupils into the public school system. This is an especially serious problem in cities with large Roman Catholic populations such as Cleveland, Buffalo and Chicago where the movement of middle-class Catholics to the suburbs has reduced the viability of central-city parochial education.

THE GEOGRAPHY OF EDUCATIONAL RESOURCES

A discussion of the resources available for the provision of education and of spatial disparities in those resources suggests that we have an accurate conception of the education production function; i.e., of the relationships between the input resources applied to education and the output of an educated citizenry. Customarily, educational resources are assumed to be economic in character and measurable in terms of expenditure per pupil, investment in libraries per pupil, in teachers per pupil, etc. Recent findings throw some doubt upon this viewpoint.

The major source of evidence in this context has been the "Coleman Report" on equality of educational opportunity.[3] This presents the findings of a federally funded inquiry into the factors affecting educational achievement where achievement is measured in terms of verbal and arithmetic skills. The achievement tests used in such studies evaluate skills that are most important in obtaining more economically rewarding jobs and, therefore, they give a good measure of the range of opportunities open to a student upon completing school.

The major conclusions as to the inputs which affect the achievement output are surprising. Of primary significance are differences in the social environment provided by the family; the social status and educational background of the family appear to be particularly important. Minority children, therefore, are unlikely to show very high achievement scores for no other reason than their deprived social and educational backgrounds.

Second in importance was the social environment provided by the school. The educational background and the aspirations of the student body were important as was the educational background and attainment of the teachers. Middle-class student bodies and teachers with middle-class backgrounds tended to have a much more positive effect on student achievement scores than did a school background which was more lower-class in character.

---

[3] James S. Coleman, et al., *Equality of Educational Opportunity,* Washington: U.S. Government Printing Office, 1966.

On the other hand, the *independent* effects of school economic resources were virtually negligible. When holding the effects of family background and school environment constant, the dollars invested per pupil had virtually no effect upon student achievement. A quotation from the Coleman Report is pertinent: "Taking all these results together one implication stands out above all: that schools bring little influence to bear on a child's achievement that is independent of his background and general social context; and this very lack of an independent effect means that the inequalities imposed on children by their home, neighborhood, and peer environment are carried along to become the inequalities with which they confront adult life at the end of school."[4]

Such results cast considerable doubt upon the orthodox wisdom and have not gone without reasonable challenge. A major problem in interpretation of the results of the analysis is that it is extremely difficult to separate out the independent effects of home environment, school environment, and resources per pupil. *Generally,* schools in which spending per pupil is higher also tend to have children largely from middle-class backgrounds. To what extent, therefore, is the large effect ascribed to home background actually due to economic resource differences from one school to another? This is a very thorny problem.

Additional criticism has focused upon a re-analysis of the data.[5] This has shown among other things that black verbal achievement scores are related to the teacher's score on a verbal facility test. It seems reasonable to suggest that differences in teacher verbal ability should be reflected in salary levels and, consequently, in expenditure per pupil. Elsewhere, and more recently, an important study of achievement levels of Michigan school children has affirmed the significant effect of school facilities, instructional materials, instructor ability, etc., when holding student and school social background constant.[6]

A more cautious viewpoint, therefore, would emphasize the roles of both social environment and economic resources in the education production function. To the extent that school environments can be varied, policy can be effective in increasing achievement levels. Each of these types of resource is considered in turn.

The availability of the resources necessary for provision of a middle-class school environment depends upon both social and institutional factors. Socially, it depends on the proportion of all children from middle-class homes who reside in a school district. In a sense, many central-city school districts are at an increasing disadvantage as their middle-class residents leave for suburban districts and are replaced by those of low social and educational background. Most suburbs, on the other hand, are largely middle class, so that theoretically the provision of a middle-class school environment for their children should be relatively easy.

---

[4] Coleman et al., op cit., p. 325.

[5] Samuel Bowles, "Towards Equality of Educational Opportunity?" *Harvard Educational Review,* vol. 38, Winter, 1968, pp. 89-99.

[6] James W. Guthrie, et al., *Schools and Inequality,* New York: The Urban Coalition, 1969.

Institutionally, on the other hand, there is the problem of the neighborhood school concept. Within school districts, children tend to be assigned to the school in their immediate neighborhood. Given residential segregation by social and racial group within a school district, schools are more likely to be uniform with respect to social class and race than diverse. Where residential segregation does not produce this outcome, the location of new schools and of school catchment boundaries can be manipulated through the political process.

Therefore, not only is there a dwindling number of middle-class children to go around in the central city, but institutional constraints minimize contact with the educationally deprived and, according to Coleman, this limits educational output. It is in this respect that the busing of pupils to achieve racial balance assumes importance. Given that blacks are largely of low-income status the chances are, all other things being equal, that busing will place black children in a much more middle-class school environment than that which they had experienced hitherto. Indeed, there is evidence that the results for achievement levels are beneficial. In Hartford, Connecticut, after two years of busing black children to white schools, the blacks had significantly improved scores on achievement while the achievement levels of the white children were unimpaired.[7] A continuing problem where busing has been introduced, however, is that of white flight to the surrounding suburbs. This clearly vitiates the aim of increasing the input of middle-class school environments into the education of lower-income children and suggests the importance of combining a busing policy with the amalgamation of central-city and suburban school districts.

When we consider economic resource problems, it is apparent that the central city is again at a disadvantage. The tax base problems of the city have already been discussed and the disadvantages of the central-city educational system emphasized. Not only are taxable capacities showing relative and, in some cases, absolute declines, but there is also the problem of *municipal overburden* with which central cities must contend. Even though central-city and suburban tax bases may be similar, less may be spent per student in the central city simply because of the greater expenditures per capita which central cities must make for police, fire service, sanitation, and public health.

State and federal aid do little to alter this generally dismal picture of inequity. In fact, quite to the contrary, they seem to have a perverse effect on the distribution of resources. At the state level, for instance, central cities generally have received appreciably less in state aid per pupil than have their respective suburban areas. On the average, and confining our attention to the 37 largest SMSAs in the U.S., we find that in the central cities the per capita (as opposed to per pupil) aid was $20.72 while in the suburban areas it was about twice that amount. A major reason for such an unegalitarian allocation resides in the formulas most state equalization procedures rely on. These were originally devised in a period when funding advantages lay more with the central city and were based

[7] James N. Miller, "What Happens After Busing Starts," *Reader's Digest*, October, 1971.

purely on a property tax base per capita criterion. What this criterion overlooks in the context of the contemporary city, however, is the problem of municipal overburden. With the possible exception of Michigan, not one state-aid system makes explicit recognition of the overburden problem.

The distribution of *federal* aid between school districts tends to reinforce this odd situation. A recent study of school districts in Michigan found that wealthy school districts with high assessed property value per pupil tended to receive as much federal aid or more than that received by poorer school districts with a lower assessed property value per pupil.[8]

THE GEOGRAPHY OF EDUCATIONAL PROVISION

The end-product of the considerations reviewed above is a demand/resource ratio for educational services which places the central city at a considerable disadvantage relative to the suburbs. This is strongly apparent in levels of expenditure per pupil; more specifically, it is reflected in disadvantageous pupil/teacher ratios, etc. As per pupil expenditures rise, the pupil/teacher ratio decreases (see Table 3.4). Funding on a more

Table 3.4. Pupil-Teacher Ratios for Selected Cities and Suburbs, 1967.

City and Suburb	Pupil-teacher ratio	Per pupil expenditures
Los Angeles	27	$ 610
Beverly Hills	17	1,192
San Francisco	26	693
Palo Alto	21	984
Chicago	28	571
Evanston	18	757
Detroit	31	530
Grosse Pointe	22	713
St. Louis City	30	525
University City	22	747
New York City	20	854
Great Neck	16	1,391
Cleveland	28	559
Cleveland Heights	22	703
Philadelphia	27	617
Lower Merion	20	733

Source: *Hearings Before the Select Committee on Equal Educational Opportunity of the United States Senate, 91st Congress, 2nd Session on Equal Educational Opportunity,   Part 6—Racial Imbalance in Urban Schools,* 1970, p. 3357.

liberal scale also would allow central-city school systems to offer a monetary counterweight to the deterring effects of working with more poorly motivated students. As it is, central-city systems have difficulty

[8] *Hearings Before the Select Committee on Equal Educational Opportunity of the U.S. Senate, 91st Congress: 2nd Session on Equal Educational Opportuntiy, Part 6—Racial Imbalance in Urban Schools,* 1970, p. 3259.

both in attracting the staff they need and in holding on to them once hired.

Frequently, the result of staff shortage is to hire teachers with less then standard certificates. In a 1968 survey of teachers, only 5.6 percent of all teachers had less than standard certificates. Large cities, however, often reported much more disturbing ratios—Chicago with 33.9 percent and Washington, D.C. with 26.0 percent, for instance.

The attrition problem is particularly critical in central-city schools. In Manhattan, one third of the teachers appointed to positions do not accept their assignments. Also, in a study of teacher attitudes in fifteen major American cities, it was found that 17 percent of all ghetto school teachers had been in their ghetto schools only one year. Such mobility is hardly conducive to a stable learning situation for the pupil.

Finally, money buys new school buildings which central-city school districts need very much. Older schools are usually larger and have larger classrooms—thus the size of classes often is larger. In ghetto areas, the problems of building need are particularly acute. As the Kerner Commission stated: because of the rapid increase in the black population which "has been concentrated in segregated neighborhoods, ghetto schools have experienced acute overcrowding. Shortages of textbooks and supplies have developed. Double shifts are common; hallways and other nonclassroom space has been adapted for classroom instruction and mobile classroom units are used. Even programs for massive construction of new schools in Negro neighborhoods cannot always keep up with increased overcrowding."[9]

Fiscal Disparities: A Quantitative Evaluation

The description above of the central-city–suburban fiscal disparities problem is in a number of respects a simplified one. First, it may not apply as much to some cities as to others; a pattern of geographical variation in the severity of the problem also may indicate something about its causes. Second, the relationships between demands, resources, and public provision presented here have been based on descriptions of others and on summary examination of tables of statistics for single variables. The anatomy of the disparities problem may not be quite that simple.

In an effort to paint a more accurate if possibly somewhat more complex picture of the fiscal disparities problem and of its geographical expression across metropolitan areas of the U.S., indices of the severity of the problem have been devised and computed for thirty-five of the largest metropolitan areas. Here we describe the empirical content of the indices, interpret them, and, on the basis of their values for different metropolitan areas, present graphical and cartographic summaries of the severity of the central-city–suburban fiscal disparities problem.

In summary, the aim has been to devise measures of fiscal constraint and/or public provision for central cities and suburbs respectively and then to compute an index of the central-city–suburban disparity or difference of these measures. The measures on which the ultimate

[9] Kerner et al., *National Advisory Commission on Civil Disorders,* Washington, D.C.: U.S. Government Printing Office, 1968, p. 432.

disparities index is based are derived from a factor analysis of twelve variables regarded as indicators of need for services, resources with which to satisfy those needs, and actual provision of public goods. The variables, along with their sources, are listed in Table 3.5.

Table 3.5. Variables, Sources of Variables and Abbreviations.

Variable No.	Variable	Source	Abbreviation of Variable
1	Percent of population, Negro, 1960	*A*, p. 39	% Negro
2	Percent of population 14 to 17 years of age not in school, 1960	*A*, p. 99	% 14-17 not in school
3	Median school years completed, persons over 25 years of age, 1960	*A*, p. 99	Median education
4	Percent of homes, owner-occupied, 1960	*A*, p. 100	% homes owner occupied
5	Percent of houses, unsound, 1960	*A*, p. 100	% houses unsound
6	Percent of labor force unemployed, 1960	*A*, p. 101	% unemployed
7	Per pupil current expenditures for local schools, 1960	*A*, p. 66	Per pupil expenditures
8	Per capita income, 1964	*A*, p. 78	Per capita income
9	Burglaries per capita, 1961	*B*	Burglaries per capita
10	Educational expenditure as a percentage of total general expenditure, 1964-65	*A*, p. 74	% educational expenditure
11	Robberies per capita, 1961	*B*	Robberies per capita
12	Per capita total local taxes as a percentage of per capita income, 1965	*A*, p. 80	Tax rate

Sources: *A*: Advisory Commission on Intergovernmental Relations, *Fiscal Balance in the American Federal System, Vol. 2: Metropolitan Fiscal Disparities,* Washington, D.C.: U.S. Government Printing Office, 1967. *B*: Federal Bureau of Investigation, *Uniform Crime Reports for the United States, 1961,* Washington, D.C.: Federal Bureau of Investigation, 1962.

Therefore, variables (such as robberies per capita) give an indication of the need for public expenditures on crime control while public safety expenditure as a percentage of total expenditure provides an indication of the burden of noneducational demands which are made on local resources. Per capita income and the extent of unsound housing give some notion of the availability of resources to apply to such public problems. Variables, such as the tax rate and per pupil expenditure, provide information on the package of public goods ultimately produced by the municipality in question.

Factor analysis of these twelve variables, however, reveals that in terms of fiscal constraint and production of public goods, cities and suburbs can be placed on two scales which are of similar importance to one another. As Table 3.6 shows, orthogonal rotation of the factors with eigenvalues greater than 1.0 to the varimax criterion produced two factors, the first accounting for 32.4 percent of the common variation and the second accounting for about 25.6 percent.

Table 3.6. Rotated Factor Loadings.

Variable	Factor I	Factor II
% Negro	.65	−.45
% 14-17 not in school	.39	−.66
Median education	−.33	.70
% homes owner-occupied	−.82	.32
% houses unsound	.42	−.74
% unemployed	.55	−.32
Per pupil expenditures	−.21	.64
Per capita income	.11	.74
Burglaries per capita	.71	−.19
% educational expenditure	−.78	.28
Robberies per capita	.84	−.25
Tax rate	.41	.21
V_ℓ^c	32.42%	25.58%

The first factor differentiates between two ideal types of municipality: Types 1A and 1B. These ideal types can be summarized as follows:

Type 1A: Blacks constitute a relatively large proportion of the total population
Low proportion of houses are owner occupied.
Relatively high proportion of houses are unsound.
High proportion of the labor force is unemployed.
Large number of burglaries per capita.
Large number of robberies per capita.
Low educational expenditure as a percentage of total expenditure.
High tax payments as a percentage of income.

Type 1B: Blacks constitute a relatively small proportion of the total population.
High proportion of houses are owner occupied.
Relatively small proportion of houses are unsound.
Low proportion of the labor force is unemployed.
Small number of burglaries per capita.
Small number of robberies per capita.
High educational expenditure as a percentage of total expenditure.
Low tax payments as a percentage of income.

In brief, the factor seems to differentiate between municipalities on the basis of their respective *burdens of demand for municipally provided public goods and services.* High unemployment, high crime rates, and large proportions of blacks create large demands for welfare services and public safety. This imposes burdens on the tax rate since, assuming income is held constant, tax payments as a proportion of income will be higher. In addition, municipal expenditures must be rearranged to cater to these more pressing needs; thus, the provision of other services such as education is likely to suffer. This is demonstrated by the low levels of educational expenditure as a proportion of total expenditure character- istic of those municipalities having a heavy burden of demands for other public goods.

Factor I, therefore, differentiates municipalities which have relatively low demand burdens from those with heavy demand burdens. That the former are largely suburban and the latter are largely central city in location is suggested by Figure 3.1. Figure 3.1 graphs the scores of SMSA suburban sections on the horizontal axis against the scores of SMSA central-city sections on the vertical axis; high burdens are indicated by high scores (the key to SMSA abbreviations is shown in Table 3.7).

Fig. 3.1 Suburban (OCC) factor scores and central-city (CC) factor scores on Factor I for thirty-five large metropolitan areas. High burdens of demand for municipal services are indicated by high factor scores while low burdens are indicated by low scores.

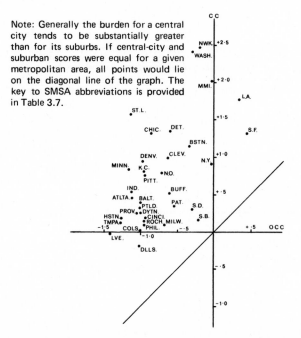

The clustering of points in the northwest quadrant of the graph is highly indicative. It suggests that the suburban sections of an SMSA tend to have a relatively reduced burden compared to the respective central- city section of the same SMSA: most SMSAs have negative scores for their suburbs and positive scores for their central-city sections. If, on the other hand, central-city scores and suburban scores were equal for a given SMSA, then all points on the graph would lie on a straight line going through the point of origin and bisecting the southwest and northeast quadrants respectively; such a line has been drawn on the graph. There is, therefore, a considerable central-city–suburban disparity in the burden of demand.

Table 3.7. Abbreviations, Burden Disparity Indices, Resource Disparity Indices and Composite Disparity Indices for 35 Large Metropolitan Areas.

Standard Metropolitan Statistical Area	Abbreviation	Burden Disparity Index	Resource Disparity Index	Composite Disparity Index
Atlanta	ATLTA.	1.54	− .51	1.98
Baltimore	BALT.	1.46	− .90	2.19
Boston	BSTN.	1.46	−1.08	2.33
Buffalo	BUFF.	1.13	−1.15	2.19
Chicago	CHIC.	2.15	−1.06	2.80
Cincinnati	CINCI.	1.15	− .76	1.88
Cleveland	CLEV.	1.65	−2.19	3.35
Columbus	COLS.	1.08	−1.60	2.57
Dallas	DLLS.	.96	− .12	1.28
Dayton	DYTN.	1.40	− .44	1.82
Denver	DENV.	1.90	.38	1.93
Detroit	DET.	1.96	− .78	2.47
Houston	HSTN.	1.42	− .42	1.83
Indianapolis	IND.	1.64	−1.33	2.63
Kansas City	K.C.	1.70	− .39	2.04
Los Angeles-Long Beach	L.A.	1.45	.15	1.56
Louisville	LVE.	1.41	− .78	2.07
Miami	MMI.	2.13	− .51	2.46
Milwaukee	MILW.	.75	−1.17	2.04
Minneapolis	MINN.	1.93	− .09	2.10
Newark	NWK.	2.67	−2.26	4.01
New Orleans	N.O.	1.50	− .61	2.01
New York	N.Y.	.95	−2.86	3.71
Paterson-Clifton-Passaic	PAT.	.90	−1.69	2.58
Philadelphia	PHIL.	1.05	−1.71	2.66
Pittsburgh	PITT.	1.89	− .50	2.25
Portland	PTLD.	1.44	.50	1.46
Providence	PROV.	1.36	.07	1.51
Rochester	ROCH.	1.13	−1.28	2.31
St. Louis	ST. L.	2.76	−1.17	3.35
San Bernardino-Riverside-Ontario	S.B.	.35	.73	.35
San Diego	S.D.	.58	− .03	.96
San Francisco-Oakland	S.F.	.87	− .35	1.39
Tampa-St. Petersburg	TMPA.	.37	.31	.56
Washington, D.C.	WASH.	2.71	− .56	3.00

This disparity in demand, however, also varies from one SMSA to another; it is apparent, for example, that while Buffalo and Detroit have very similar burdens in their suburban sections, their central-city burdens are rather different, with Detroit having the greater disparity. A measure of this disparity can be provided simply by subtracting the suburban score from the central-city score; these indices of *burden disparity* for different SMSAs are presented in Table 3.7.

It is hardly surprising to find some of the SMSAs with very large burden disparities. St. Louis, Washington, D.C., and Newark are clear candidates for first place and Chicago is not far behind; rather surprisingly Miami also appears to have a serious disparity problem. At the other end of the scale, the presence of New York City and the Paterson-Passaic SMSA is unexpected. Clearly, the central-city–suburban fiscal disparity problem in the New York City area must derive more from factors related to the availability of taxable resources.

Possibly of greater interest than the simple tabulation of burden disparity indices is a mapping. This is accomplished in Figure 3.2 with a categorization of disparity indices into four groups of quartiles. The most interesting feature of the map is the confinement of the worst of the burden disparity problem to the Northeast segments of the nation; cities in the South—with the exception of Miami—and on the West Coast seem relatively less affected.

Turning to the second factor identified by our analysis we find a quite different polarity of ideal-type municipalities. These are referred to as Types 2A and 2B:

> Type 2A: Blacks constitute a relatively small proportion of total population.
> A low proportion of the population aged 14-17 is not in school.
> High median education.
> High proportion of houses are structurally sound.
> High per pupil school expenditures.
> High per capita income.
>
> Type 2B: Blacks constitute a relatively large proportion of the total population.
> Large proportion of the population aged 14-17 is not in school.
> Low median education.
> Low proportion of houses are structurally sound.
> Low per pupil school expenditures.
> Low per capita income.

The differentiation of this factor seems to be in terms of *the resources available for meeting the burden of public demands.* Those of higher income tend to occupy higher-value properties from which the tax yield is commensurately greater; in addition, they provide more public revenue in the form of those sales taxes which have a progressive rather than a regressive incidence. Structurally sound properties also are assessed at higher values than structurally unsound properties, again providing an additional bonus for the public coffers. The availability of resources permits greater spending on those goods and demand for which is more tax-resource elastic—education is a case in point. Other variables, such as median income which load highly on this factor, are simply correlates of high per capita income.

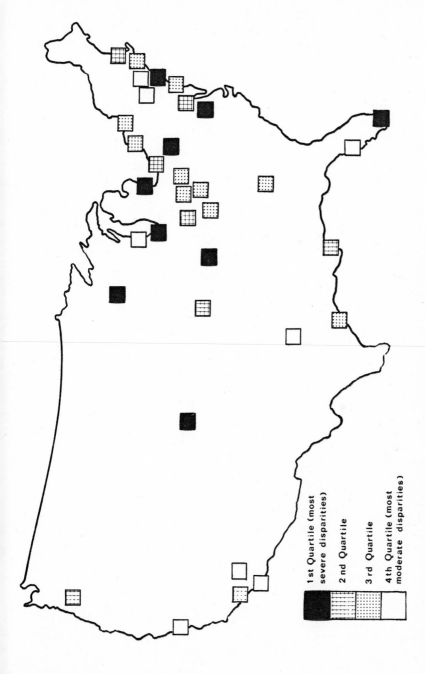

Fig. 3.2 The geography of burden disparity indices for thirty-five large metropolitan areas. The burden disparity problem tends to be greatest for metropolitan areas in the Northeastern section of the nation.

The differentiation has been made, therefore, between municipalities which have relatively ample resources from which to finance public goods and services and municipalities which have relatively meager resources for such purposes. Again, as with Factor I, there is some correlation between resource status and location in a metropolitan area. Generally, it would appear that the central city of an SMSA tends to be resource meager while the suburban section of the same SMSA is resource rich.

In Figure 3.3, central-city scores have been plotted on the vertical axis, while suburban scores are plotted on the horizontal axis; negative scores indicate resource weakness. If the suburbs of an SMSA had the same resource availability as the central city of that SMSA, then all points would lie on the indicated line. Clearly, most of the points assume a position to the southeast of this line; thus, for most SMSAs, suburban resource availability considerably exceeds central-city resource availability. A resource disparity index has been computed for each SMSA and scores on this index are presented in Table 3.7.

Fig. 3.3 Suburban (OCC) factor scores and central-city (CC) factor scores on Factor II for thirty-five large metropolitan areas. Low (i.e., negative) factor scores indicate a weakness in the availability of resources for financing the municipal production of public goods.

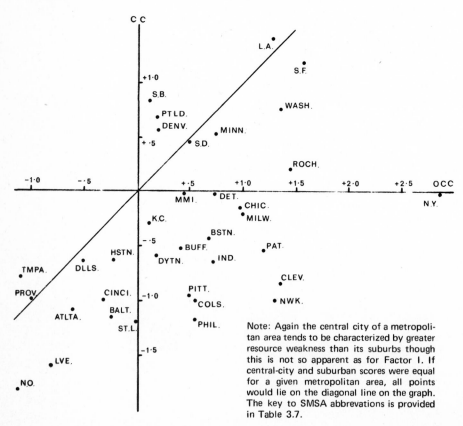

Note: Again the central city of a metropolitan area tends to be characterized by greater resource weakness than its suburbs though this is not so apparent as for Factor I. If central-city and suburban scores were equal for a given metropolitan area, all points would lie on the diagonal line on the graph. The key to SMSA abbreviations is provided in Table 3.7.

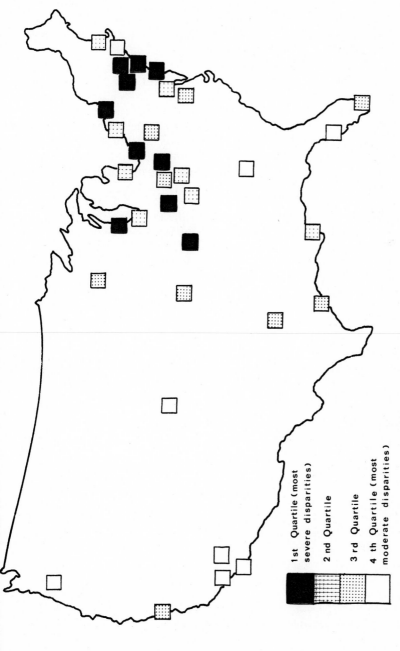

Fig. 3.4 The geography of resource disparity indices for thirty-five large metropolitan areas. The resource disparity problem also tends to be greatest for metropolitan areas in the Northeastern section of the U.S.; Western and Southern metropolitan areas appear to have problems of a relatively minor nature.

New York City is quite clearly the SMSA with the greatest central-city–suburban resource disparity; Newark also has a critically high score to compound the problems created by a high score on the burden disparity index. Cities with disparity indices which favor the central city rather than the suburbs tend to be located largely in the South and on the West Coast.

This latter fact is brought out rather effectively by the map of resource disparity indices shown in Figure 3.4. The problems of the Northeast are now much more in evidence with all the largest SMSAs appearing in the two highest quartiles. In contrast, the West Coast and the South appear to be havens of central-city–suburb resource equity.

Quite apparently, however, the disparities problem is not one of either *burden disparity* or *resource disparity*—it is compounded of both. In order to obtain some measure of the overall severity of the disparities problem, therefore, a *composite disparity index* was computed on the basis of both the burden disparity index and the resource disparity index.[10] SMSA scores on this composite index are shown in Table 3.7 and the cartographic plotting is presented in Figure 3.5.

Figure 3.5 heavily underlines the fact that the fiscal disparities problem is largely a problem of the Northeast and the Midwest: New York City, Chicago, Cleveland, Philadelphia, Washington, D.C., and Newark all appear in the first quartile. In contradistinction, in the South and West only Miami appears outside of the bottom two quartiles; on the West Coast, all five SMSAs are in the bottom quartile on the composite disparity index. Why this distinctive geographic pattern exists is not immediately apparent. Possibly it is related to the greater physical extent of many Western and Southern cities. Much of the population growth of these SMSAs took place at a time when annexation by the central city was facilitated, unlike the situation in the Northeast and Midwest; this has meant that central cities in the West and South have been able to expand areally and obtain tracts of suburban land. Yet another factor may be the reduced numbers of blacks in Western central cities and their relatively low levels of criminal activity in cites of the South. There is clearly a plethora of hypotheses which could benefit from empirical tests.

---

[10] Thus far we have employed the statistical distance between suburban and central city factor scores on one single factor or dimension to derive a disparity index for a given SMSA. This idea can be extended to the statistical distance between suburb and central city factor scores on two factors or dimensions: $\sqrt{X_1^2 + X_2^2}$ where X_1 is the statistical distance on Factor 1 for a given SMSA and X_2 is the statistical distance on Factor 2 for the same SMSA. In order to be meaningful in this case, however, the distances X_1 and X_2 must be based on scales which are uniform as to sign both within scales and between scales. In this particular case, this is not so: the statistical distances on Factor 2, therefore, were transformed into positive scores by multiplication by a constant of -1 and the addition of a constant of .73 to the result.

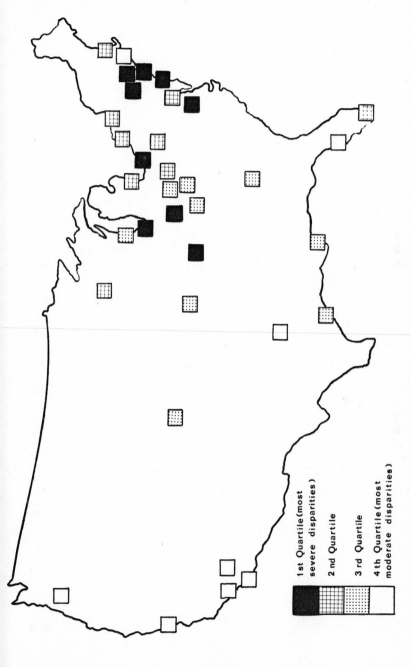

Fig. 3.5 The geography of the central-city-suburban fiscal disparities problem. This map is based on the composite disparity index discussed in the text. The Northeastern – Western and Southern regional dichotomy is clearly apparent.

1 st Quartile (most severe disparities)

2 nd Quartile

3 rd Quartile

4 th Quartile (most moderate disparities)

Table 3.8. Percent of Population Living in Non-Southern Metropolitan Areas*
Born in the South, 1960.

Metropolitan Area*	White	Negro	Total
New England:			
SMSAs	1.51	1.04	2.55
Middle Atlantic:			
SMSAs	2.00	4.18	6.18
Center city of SMSAs		7.45	
East North Central:			
SMSAs	5.66	6.49	12.15
Center city of SMSAs		12.01	
West North Central:			
SMSAs	4.76	3.61	8.37
Pacific:			
SMSAs	9.21	3.50	12.71
Center city of SMSAs		9.42	

*SMSAs with populations of over one million only.

Source: J. F. Kain, and J. Persky, "The North's Stake in Southern Poverty," in *Rural Poverty in the United States*, Washington, D.C.: U.S. Government Printing Office, 1968, p. 293.

An Analysis of the Fiscal Disparities Problem

In the first section of this chapter, we have described an increasing geographical polarization of public provision between independent suburbs and central city. To what mechanisms can we ascribe this polarization? This is a very difficult problem. In the city, everything is related to everything else. It is extremely difficult to characterize the situation as anything but a cobweb of cause-and-effect relationships in which causes at one point in time become effects at a later point in time in an intricate series of interlaced feedback effects.

It is clear, however, that the links which make up these congeries of interactions occur at at least two geographical levels: (1) that of the nation as a whole in which metropolitan areas are linked to the more rural areas of the nation and (2) that of the metropolitan area as a whole in which the central city is linked to its surrounding ring of independent suburbs. Our purpose now is to examine the problem of central-city-suburban disparities in public provision at these two geographical scales. The interrelationships of events at diverse scales sould then be apparent.

The National Context

At the national level, the major relevant linkage is the migration to the larger metropolitan areas of poor, undereducated, and often unemployable people from the South and Appalachia. For a variety of reasons, most of this migration of the poor terminates in central cities rather than in independent suburbs. This is partly related to the locational patterns of lower-income housing in metropolitan areas; it is also due to discrimination in the mechanisms by which housing is allocated.

The data documenting this movement and the deficient skills of its members leave much to be desired; from the viewpoint of formulating mitigating policies, the Bureau of the Census should collect a far more adequate body of data than presently exists. Nevertheless, a crude quantitative picture can be sketched. Table 3.8 presents for non-Southern SMSAs the proportion of the population which was born in the South. The figures given for central cities for blacks are based on the reasonable assumption that all black migrants from the South who terminate in these SMSAs, located in central cities.[11] The most important feature of this table is that central cities in the Middle Atlantic, East North Central, and Pacific seem to be the most affected by the black Southern migration: this includes such cities as New York City, Newark, Philadelphia, Baltimore, Washington, Pittsburgh, Cleveland, Chicago, Detroit, Cincinnati, Los Angeles, and San Francisco.

Table 3.9. Percentage of Native Born Heads of Households with Given Levels of Education by Race and Region of Birth: North-Central Region.

Residence and schooling	Born in South			Born in rest of country		
	Negro	*White*	*All*	*Negro*	*White*	*All*
Entire region:						
Less than 5 years	21.5	9.3	13.7	7.7	2.9	3.0
8 years or less	62.5	51.7	55.7	35.4	36.2	36.2
Some college	5.8	12.5	10.1	9.6	18.5	18.3
SMSAs greater than						
1 million, entire SMSA:						
Less than 5 years	20.2	5.2	13.3	7.5	2.1	2.4
8 years or less	60.9	42.8	52.5	31.8	28.9	29.0
Some college	5.8	16.5	10.8	9.2	22.8	22.2
Central cities:						
Less than 5 years	19.1	5.1	15.0	7.0	2.6	2.9
8 years or less	59.9	44.9	55.5	28.5	33.8	33.4
Some college	6.7	13.9	8.8	9.5	19.1	18.4

Source: J. F. Kain and J. Persky, "The North's Stake in Southern Poverty," in *Rural Poverty in the United States,* Washington, D.C.: U.S. Government Printing Office, 1968, p. 295.

That these Southern-born migrants bring with them inadequate education and job skills and impose commensurately large demands on the poverty-related services of central cities outside the South is apparent from another set of tabulations. However, the data upon which these tabulations are based are even less ideal than those used for the other tabulations; thus, for this reason, the presentations are limited to data for the North Central (East and West) region (the destination of the largest number of blacks migrating from the South).

Table 3.9 presents evidence on the schooling of migrants, black and white alike, from the South. The table classifies migrants in terms of the three dimensions of race, locational origin (South or rest of country), and

[11] John F. Kain and Joseph J. Persky, "The North's Stake in Southern Rural Poverty," in *Rural Poverty in the United States,* Washington, D.C.: U.S. Government Printing Office, 1968, pp. 293-294.

locational destination (the region as a whole, SMSAs with over a million people and central cities). Within each group of migrants, the proportions of group members having received given amounts of education are indicated. It is evident, therefore, that migrants from the South, irrespective of race, are considerably less educated than are migrants from the remainder of the nation. For all migrants terminating in central cities, 55.5 percent of those born in the South received only eight years of education or less while the corresponding proportion for those born elsewhere in the nation is a much lower 33.4 percent. Conversely, 18.4 percent of all migrants from outside the South have had some college education while the figure for migrants from the South is only 8.8 percent.

A second feature of the table is that black migrants to central cities, irrespective of regional origin, are even more educationally disadvantaged and black migrants from the South terminating in large SMSAs are the most disadvantaged of all—20.2 percent have had less than five years of education and only 5.8 percent have any college education. Compare this with the corresponding proportions for whites from the rest of the nation—2.1 percent and 2.8 percent respectively.

The effects of these educational differences are apparent in the Census Bureau's small sample (1 in 1,000) data on poverty households. Confining our attention still to the North Central region and defining the poverty line as $3,000 for families, it has been found that *over one-third of all individuals classified as falling below the poverty line in large SMSAs belong to families in which the family head originated in the South.* Twenty-five percent of all the poverty persons belong to households headed by Southern-born blacks.

To the extent that the limited data permit, therefore, it seems possible to trace a link between the migration of poor Southerners, particularly Southern blacks, to Northern cities and the relatively high demand in central cities of the North for poverty-linked services. This has obvious effects on the ability of Northern cities to fund other services such as education.

Central-city governments are powerless to stem this migration and, consequently, to remedy their fiscal problems. A number of central cities have attempted to impose residency requirements for receipt of welfare payments but these have been struck down by the Supreme Court on constitutional grounds. The root cause of the problem, however, lies not so much in the inability of central cities to control this clearly detrimental movement but in the low investments made in the education of the migrants. For many, their education has left them ill-prepared for the occupational demands of Northern cities—the result is unemployment or a low-paying job and poverty. Largely responsible for the low levels of investment in education are the Southern school districts from which the migrants originate. Per pupil expenditures in Southern states are appreciably below those of the U.S. as a whole. During 1964-65, current expenditures per pupil in the Southern states were only 76 percent of the U.S. average. This is a considerable improvement over the much lower 64.4 percent during 1929-30, but it still represents an educational disadvantage for the Southerner. Also, it almost certainly understates the disadvantages of the Southern black who has historically been given much less ample education facilities than his white counterpart.

This is not to say that there is any lack of tax effort in the Southern states for the totality of school children. Their tax efforts often have exceeded those of Northern states. Rather, low educational investment in the South is largely a result of the relative poverty of the area; the states simply cannot afford to spend more. The result, however, has been the imposition of negative externalities upon Northern central cities with serious implications for the problem of central-city–suburban fiscal disparities.

The Metropolitan Context

Within metropolitan areas, the context of jurisdictional fragmentation assumes great importance. Consider the locational behavior of households and firms. Two economic roles are involved: that of the consumer of public services and that of the taxpayer footing the bill for those services. Generally, households and firms have tended to arrange themselves locationally so that the ratio of demand for services to tax capacity tends to be relatively high in the central city and relatively low in suburban municipalities. This produces the fiscal disparity problem noted above and is a major reason for the strong inequalities of public provision which exist between central city and suburbs. The distribution of educational expenditure, pollution, police protection, and taxation rate, therefore, are all at issue here.

This initial characterization of the problems of the fragmented metropolitan area leads to the more critical question: why do people arrange themselves in the way that they have and what are the forces resisting a locational arrangement likely to produce greater equity in public provision across the municipalities of a metropolitan area?

A second characterization of the problems of unequal public provision, however, would point out the effect of intermunicipal movements on the demand for public services. The demand for public services within a municipality consists not only of the demands of people who reside there, but also of those who move through or work in or recreate there. Clearly, what is involved here is a negative externality problem—while a municipality may produce a service for the consumption of its residents, it is very difficult to exclude nonresidents from use of many of those services. Where municipalities as a result of such movement impose negative externalities of a similar magnitude on each other, there will be no impact upon the geography of public provision across municipalities. If, however, movements are asymmetric and negative spillovers are proportionately greater in one direction than in another, there may be serious effects upon the locational incidence of public provision.

In summary, in explaining inequalities of public provision between central city and independent suburb we need to ask two questions. First, why have households and firms located in such a way as to produce a high ratio of demand to tax capacity in the central city and a low ratio in the independent suburb? Second, what are the effects of movement between city and suburb on that inequality?

THE LOCATIONAL ARRANGEMENT OF HOUSEHOLDS AND FIRMS IN THE FRAGMENTED METROPOLITAN CONTEXT

Movement Constraints. Elsewhere, migratory choices resulting in permanent residence have been ascribed to three major considerations: (1) movement costs, (2) attractiveness or place utility, and (3) the locational structure of movement opportunities.[12] Given the limited areal scope of metropolitan areas, it is unlikely that movement costs are a constraining factor in residential choice. Attractiveness and the locational structure of movement opportunities, however, appear to be of critical significance.

The attraction of the suburbs for resident and firm alike is so widely known that it requires little additional comment here. For firms, there are the advantages of low land costs and proximity to suburbanizing markets and labor forces; for the household, there is a host of environmental advantages ranging from low density occupancy and an often quasi-rural ambience to the quality of suburban schools, the absence of busing to achieve racial integration of schools, and greater physical security.

Although most citizens evaluate suburban municipalities considerably more positively than central-city locations, suburban locations do not provide opportunities for all. It is apparent that poorer populations and black populations have shown a slow rate of movement to the suburbs relative to their middle-class and white counterparts. Similar disparities have been noted in the case of dirty industry vis-à-vis the more rapidly suburbanizing clean industry. For a number of reasons, the suburban location is a movement opportunity for only a limited segment of the urban population. A variety of institutional and economic barriers tends to confine the locational choice of the poor, the black, and the polluting industries to the central city by making suburban property prohibitively costly or merely prohibitive for them. These barriers assume the following major forms: (1) exclusionary zoning, (2) discriminatory markets, and (3) high property values. Each is discussed in turn.

Exclusionary Zoning: The power to zone land for different uses is vested in the individual municipalities making up a metropolitan area. This zoning power covers both the intensity of land use and the specific type of activity (e.g., type of industry) to be carried out on a piece of land. It is perfectly feasible, therefore, for suburban municipalities to "zone in" clean industry and to "zone out" dirty industry. Indeed, this is carried on widely, thus imposing the burden of continuing air pollution on central-city populations.

The zoning ordinance, therefore, gives a municipality great power to affect the residential movement of people and the movement of industry between central city and independent suburb and, indeed, the more interesting effects are residential. Undeveloped residential land can be zoned in such a way that only higher-income groups will be able to afford

[12] Kevin R. Cox, *Man, Location and Behavior: An Introduction to Human Geography*, New York: John Wiley, 1972.

the developed properties. The use of zoning in this manner is of major significance in explaining the continuing inability of blacks and poor whites to suburbanize. As should now be apparent, some types of residents impose heavy demands on local public services relative to their contribution to the tax capacity of the municipality. Such is the lower-income citizen with, say, two children to educate. Almost certainly, he will be limited in his housing choice to an extremely modest home unlikely to yield a high property tax. By locating in a wealthier municipality, therefore, the resident will be imposing negative externalities on the other residents, since his unfavorable service-need/tax-capacity ratio implies some fiscal redistribution by the rest of the community.

By zoning for a large minimal lot size, however, the price of subsequent residential property in the municipality can be maintained at a high level, thus ensuring a fairly favorable service-need/tax-capacity ratio. In Cuyahoga, County, surrounding Cleveland, two-thirds of the underdeveloped land zoned for single family residential construction in the late 1960s was zoned for minimum lots of half an acre. In adjacent Geauga County, 85 percent of residentially zoned land had to be developed with single family homes on lots of an acre or more.[13] Under such circumstances, even if a modest home is built on the lot, the original aim of minimizing the service-need/tax-capacity ratio will have been partly achieved since the large lot will carry a proportionately higher assessment, and there will be fewer houses and, therefore, fewer children from such modest homes to educate.

An alternative zoning strategy which satisfies the same purpose is that of zoning for single family residences rather than for multifamily residences such as those represented by the apartment developments of public housing sponsors. In the 1960s, therefore, less than 1 percent of residentially zoned, developed land in the New York City suburbs was zoned for multifamily housing.[14]

Minimal lot size and single family residence zoning not only restrict the entry of the poorer population; since most blacks are poor, it also has the effect of keeping the suburbs white. This not only is seen as a desirable end by white suburban populations, but it also contributes towards the goal of maximizing the service-need/tax-capacity ratio, because according to current mythology property values (and hence tax capacity) fall with the residential proximity of blacks.

That zoning ordinances are indeed employed in this discriminatory manner is evident from the chronology of their application. Their use is often elicited by the threat of some projected high-density and/or low-income housing development. An example of such a threat-zoning sequence has been provided more recently by the actions of the small suburban community of Blackjack, Missouri in the St. Louis area. Early in 1970, a nonprofit corporation organized by the Methodist Church in St. Louis drew up plans to construct, with federal subsidy, townhouses for lower-income groups in the then unincorporated community of Blackjack at a density of just over eight per acre. Later that year, after the

[13] Joseph P. Fried, *Housing Crisis, U.S.A.*, New York: Praeger, 1971, p. 48.
[14] Ibid., pp. 48-49.

announcement of these construction plans, the community incorporated and obtained the power to zone; two months later the new city of Blackjack rezoned the projected building site so as to impose a minimum lot size of one-third of an acre—thus effectively quashing the project.[15]

Building codes and subdivision regulations are often used for a similar discriminatory purpose by suburban municipalities attempting to resist the development of their vacant residential land by or for lower-income groups from the central cities. Building codes, for example, can raise the price of houses by insisting on particularly expensive methods of construction. Alternatively, subdivision regulations can substitute for minimal lot zoning by specifying an especially large distance between the street and the house.

The locational effects of such exclusionary zoning and building code practices are much more widespread than might at first be imagined. Regulation in one municipality can raise the price of building land in adjacent unregulated municipalities, thus immunizing them also from high-density, low-income housing developments. The implications of such policies for congestion in central cities can easily be imagined. Home prices increase, thus stimulating subdivision into apartments, overcrowding, and health problems. Not the least, the general fiscal disparity problem is further aggravated. The Ford automobile plant in Mahwah, New Jersey, for example, employs 4,200 workers; only 2 percent of these live within the municipal boundaries while many of the others commute from Newark and New York City. The local property taxes from the automobile plant are, of course, paid solely to Mahwah. So successful is the municipality's policy of exclusionary zoning along with its policy of attracting industry that in 1970 the tax rate on industrial and commercial property was only 1.55 percent of full value. Yet, in nearby Newark, where almost 1,000 of Ford's black workers are housed and educated, the tax rate was 7.14 percent of full value—itself a tribute to the desertion of central cities by businesses contributing large amounts to property taxes.[16]

Discriminatory Housing Markets: The residential mobility of blacks relative to whites is handicapped by factors other than zoning regulations which serve to keep low-income housing out of the suburbs. Specifically, and despite much recent legislation to the contrary, housing markets in American cities continue to be discriminatory with respect to race: willingness of whites to sell a property or to be a party to the sale of a property in a dominantly white residential district is highly contingent upon the race of the buyer. This dual housing market undoubtedly reflects the neighborhood preferences of whites.

The dual housing market, though originally sanctified by government actions now defunct, is perpetuated by a variety of informal mechanisms. Some of these as they operate in the Washington, D.C. area were recently identified at a Senate hearing.[17] Apparently there is a tendency to shift to

[15] *New York Times,* November 15, 1970.
[16] P. Davidoff, L. Davidoff and N. N. Gold, "The Suburbs Have to Open Their Gates," *New York Times Magazine,* November 7, 1971.
[17] *Hearings Before the Select Committee on Equal Educational Opportunity of the U.S. Senate, 91st Congress: 2nd Session on Equal Educational Opportunity, Part 5—De Facto Segregation and Housing Discrimination,* 1970, pp. 2945-2966.

strategies which explicitly discriminate on economic grounds, though which, therefore, implicitly discriminate on racial grounds. Some real estate agents will not rent apartments to persons whose wages are on an hourly scale; only salaried employees are eligible. Sales and rental agents also are nonaggressive in pursuing black prospects and frequently maintain false waiting lists for properties as a means of implementing discriminatory allocations of housing.

Dual housing markets exert very potent effects upon the availability of suburban residential opportunities to blacks. Generally, whites are willing to sell property to blacks only where the pertinent housing is located in an area experiencing or likely to experience racial change. Since the ghetto tends to expand at its edge, most such areas are located close to the ghetto.[18] Given that the ghetto tends to be distant from the independent suburbs, the sale of suburban property to blacks is unusual.

The record to date of the recently instituted "Section 235 Housing Program" provides interesting confirmation of the continuation of a dual housing market and its effect on the exclusion of blacks from the suburbs. The program known as Section 235 is a federal program of subsidized home ownership for low-income families and was introduced as part of a broader package of housing legislation in 1968. In essence, it provides subsidies in the form of interest reduction payments to mortgage lenders on behalf of lower-income purchasers to enable them to purchase and own their own homes. There are statutory income limits on participation and housing cannot cost more than $18,000 (or $21,000 in some high-cost areas of the nation). The housing unit purchases either can be new, built specifically for Section 235 purchasers, or existing housing.

The program is particularly interesting since, by its restriction to lower-income families, it does hold relatively constant a critical variable affecting housing choice. It has often been claimed, for example, that blacks are ghettoized because they are largely low income. Examination of purchase patterns under the program, therefore, might confirm this notion.

In 1970, such an examination was carried out on a sample of purchases in the cities of Little Rock, Philadelphia, St. Louis, and Denver under the auspices of the U.S. Civil Rights Commission.[19] Table 3.10 presents some of the information collected by the commission. The most pertinent facts to be derived from this table are: (1) most blacks—over 75 percent of them—who purchased housing under Section 235 purchased it in the central city; over 88 percent of the white purchasers, on the other hand, moved into suburban housing; (2) almost all *new* housing purchased was in the suburbs while over 70 percent of the *existing* housing purchased was in the central city. Given the availability of building land, the latter is only to be expected. When taken in conjunction with the first finding, however, it suggests that blacks, due to purchases in the central city, have been largely confined to existing housing while whites have been able to purchase new housing. Only 2 to 3 percent of black purchasers, for

[18] Richard L. Morrill, "The Negro Ghetto: Problems and Alternatives," *Geographical Review*, vol. 55, no. 2, July, 1965, pp. 339-361.
[19] U.S. Commission on Civil Rights, *Home Ownership for Lower Income Families*, Washington, D.C.: U.S. Government Printing Office, 1971.

Table 3.10. Classification of Housing Units Purchased Under Section 235 According to Age of Housing, Location of Housing and Race of Buyer. *

	Black Buyers		White Buyers		
	Suburb	Central City	Suburb	Central City	Total
New housing	1	2	74	0	77
Existing housing	24	75	10	10	119
Subtotal	25	77	84	10	196
Total	102		94		

* Based on a sample of buyers in Philadelphia, St. Louis, Denver and Little Rock, 1970.

Source: U.S. Commission on Civil Rights, *Home Ownership for Lower-Income Families,* Washington, D.C.: U.S. Government Printing Office, 1971, p. 16.

example, moved into new housing; this contrasts with over 78 percent of the white purchasers.

The different locational patterns of black and white purchases under Section 235 are demonstrated particularly clearly for the city of Little Rock (see Figure 3.6). Apparently, most whites have purchased new housing and this has been to a large extent in suburban locations. Most blacks, on the other hand, have purchased existing housing and this largely in areas experiencing racial transition or in the existing ghetto.

The Commission found that a major contributory factor to this locational pattern was the racially discriminatory manner in which the program operated. This in turn depended on the lack of sophistication of the purchaser. The typical Section 235 buyer, for instance, often lacked basic information regarding eligibility or the location of housing available for purchase under the Section 235 program. Major sources of information were real estate brokers and newspaper advertisements. Real estate brokers, it was found, however, often steered the purchaser into locations which they believed most appropriate for the buyer's racial or ethnic background. The purchaser was usually offered little choice and discriminatory allocation was facilitated by a take-it-or-leave-it attitude on the part of the broker.

Newspaper advertisements were little better from the viewpoint of intentionally structuring the residential choice situation in a racially discriminatory manner. In one city visited by the Commission, for example, advertisements often used such expressions as "Anyone Can Buy" or simply "Anyone" as a cue to encourage blacks and warn whites. As a consequence, Section 235 has done little to alter existing patterns of residential location by race.

It is possible, of course, that the resultant housing allocation is what blacks want; i.e., they prefer ghetto locations. This is a viewpoint commonly expressed in the real estate industry. Nearly all brokers interviewed by the U.S. Civil Rights Commission in the survey discussed here were convinced that blacks, especially low-income blacks, do not

Fig. 3.6 Section 235 home purchases by location and race in Little Rock, Arkansas. (Source: U.S. Commission on Civil Rights, *Home Ownership for Lower Income Families*, Washington, D.C.: United States Government Printing Office, 1972, pp. 27-28.)

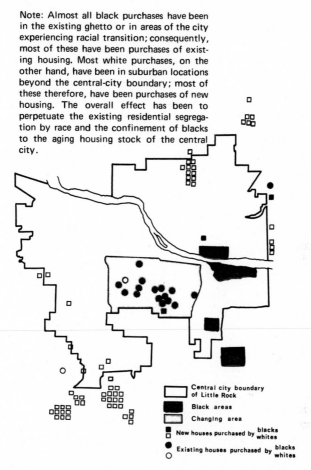

Note: Almost all black purchases have been in the existing ghetto or in areas of the city experiencing racial transition; consequently, most of these have been purchases of existing housing. Most white purchases, on the other hand, have been in suburban locations beyond the central-city boundary; most of these therefore, have been purchases of new housing. The overall effect has been to perpetuate the existing residential segregation by race and the confinement of blacks to the aging housing stock of the central city.

Central city boundary of Little Rock

Black areas

Changing area

New houses purchased by blacks whites

Existing houses purchased by blacks whites

want to move into predominantly white neighborhoods. However, there is evidence that this is just not so. An experimental counseling project conducted by a private group in Indianapolis during 1967-68 is instructive in this regard.[20]

The project used voluntary counselors and showed FHA-acquired properties throughout the city to inner-city families who were being relocated due to urban renewal, displacement by highway construction, etc. It was found that for the blacks among these families, neighborhood racial composition was of very limited importance in residential choice. Therefore, out of 38 black families, 20 selected homes in white neighborhoods, 4 selected homes in racially changing areas of the city, and 14 selected homes in black neighborhoods.

[20] Daniel J. Baum, *Toward a Free Housing Market*, Miami: University of Miami Press, 1971.

The implications of a relaxation of the dual housing market structure for the residential location patterns of blacks are quite staggering in their magnitude. Using 1960 data, calculations have been made for eleven large metropolitan areas to predict the residential locations of black households if, at every income level, identical proportions of blacks and whites were homeowners and identical proportions of blacks and whites in both owner and tenant categories lived in the suburbs.[21] As a summary statistic, it was found that 40 percent of all blacks would reside in the suburbs; compare this with the actual 1960 figure of 16 percent.

Property Values: While institutional barriers (such as building codes and zoning regulations) are effective in minimizing the service-demand/tax-capacity ratio, further barriers of an economic nature interpose themselves between the poorer inner-city residents and the suburbs. We have already remarked on the effects of minimal lot size zoning regulations on land prices in adjacent municipalities lacking such regulations. It seems, however, that there is a much more general economic factor working against the locational aspirations of the poor. Generally, the availability of environmental advantages in suburban locations—particularly the reputedly good schools, low housing densities, and access to open countryside—increases the demand for properties in such locations and, consequently, increases their value beyond the level at which low-income groups can afford them.

This is exemplified by a recent study of property values across approximately fifteen municipalities in northeast New Jersey, all lying within the New York metropolitan region.[22] Empirically, the study attempts to identify the effects of local property taxes and public expenditures on local property values in an effort to isolate evidence consistent with a theory that public provision advantages will be reflected in a bidding up of property values. It is apparent, however, that property values are also affected by other variables such as accessibility to employment, the physical character of the residential properties, and of the general area; these variables are very carefully taken into account in the study. Employing the critical educational variable—expenditure per pupil—as the measure of public expenditure, the study presents the important conclusions that property values do indeed: (1) increase with increasing public expenditure and (2) increase with decreasing tax rates. On the average, when holding public expenditures constant, an increase of local tax rates by one percentage point serves to reduce the market value of property by about $1,500.

In summary, what this analysis suggests is that the effects of institutional barriers to movement (such as those implicit in exclusionary zoning and building code restrictions) over the long term have a double-barrelled effect. First, they serve to restrict construction of low-income housing on

---

[21] John F. Kain, "Theories of Residential Location and Realities of Race," Program on Regional and Urban Economics, Discussion Paper No. 47, Harvard University, June, 1969.
[22] Wallace E. Oates, "The Effects of Property Taxes and Local Public Spending on Property Values: An Empirical Study of Tax Capitalization and the Tiebout Hypothesis," *Journal of Political Economy,* vol. 77, November-December, 1969, pp. 957-971.

vacant land in the suburbs. Second, such restriction gives the independent suburb a very favorable service-demand/tax-capacity ratio permitting it to offer an attractive tax rate and expenditure package. In its turn, this greater attractiveness induces a bidding up of prices of existing properties, thereby reducing again the housing opportunities open to lower-income groups from the central city.

The Negative Externality Effects of Movement Constraints. Quite clearly, the barriers to movement which independent suburbs impose on the poor of the central city must be regarded as a major factor in the genesis of the central-city–suburban fiscal disparities problem in general and the central-city fiscal crisis in particular. The whole structure of movement constraints filters to the suburbs those who add to fiscal surplus and keeps penned up in the city those who detract. The suburban localization of those who add to fiscal surplus allows the suburb to reduce its tax rate for a given level of public provision which makes it still more attractive to central-city residents. Those who can meet the requirements of the suburban filter suburbanize. Those who cannot meet the requirements stay in the central city. The process compounds the fiscal problem of the central city, therefore, at the same time as it enhances the fiscal prospects of the suburb.

In addition, it is possible to trace other chains of cause-and-effect linking these movement constraints to the reduced welfare of the central-city resident. Many of these effects are experienced to a different degree by middle-class and lower-class residents; as a consequence, the demand for poverty-linked services in the central city increases and aggravates the fiscal disparities problem further. Here we treat four of the more obvious and more documented negative externalities imposed by suburbs on central-city populations: (1) the redistribution of power from lower-income consumers of public goods to higher-income consumers, (2) central-city urban renewal and highway construction programs, (3) the housing costs of central-city, lower-income groups and (4) reduction of lower-income group access to employment.

The Redistribution of Power from Lower-Income Consumers of Public Goods to Higher-Income Consumers: Lower- and middle-income groups have differential abilities to move out of the central city *and* differential abilities to provide positive externalities in the form of higher property values. Together with a deteriorating central-city fiscal situation, this provides an ideal context for a transfer of power from lower class to middle class.

Middle-income groups, unlike lower-income groups, can easily relocate out of the central city into independent suburbs. Their relocation, however, imposes at least two negative externalities on the city: (1) their residential places will probably be taken by lower-income groups who will provide an increased burden on municipal services and (2) such lower-income households are less likely to maintain or improve the property and, therefore, maintain or increase its assessed evaluation; rather, the end of this filtering process is likely to be property abandonment and the loss of all tax revenue. Alternatively, the middle-class resident provides positive externalities to the central city in the form of reduced demand for certain municipal services (for instance, reduced crime leading to a reduced demand for police) and in the form of maintained or increased property values. These positive externalities are valued higher as the fiscal situation of the central city deteriorates.

In these circumstances, a premium is likely to be placed on municipal policies which encourage the middle class to stay in the central city. Such policies in a manner which benefits the higher-income relative to the schools so that schools in middle-class neighborhoods receive benefits in the form of more experienced teachers, a wider range of curricula offerings, or a catchment area gerrymandered to exclude blacks. Alternatively, there may be an adjustment of municipal taxation and expenditure policies in a manner which benefits the higher income relative to the lower-income groups; an examination of the ratio of gross assessed value to sales price for housing in different price brackets might be highly revealing in the context of central cities under varying degrees of fiscal constraint.

It is highly likely, therefore, that differential movement capabilities impose negative externalities on central-city, lower-income groups by increasing the ability of the central-city middle class to influence public policy in their favor and to the detriment of lower-income groups.

Central-City Urban Renewal and Highway Construction Programs: A direct consequence of the central-city fiscal crisis and indirectly, therefore, of barriers to the mobility of lower-income groups have been policies designed ostensibly to lure back the middle-class resident and the erstwhile patron of downtown business.

Urban renewal policies, for instance, for which very large federal subsidies are available, have been used as an instrument for replacing low assessed value properties occupied by low-income groups by much higher assessed value properties necessarily occupied by middle-class residents. Urban freeway construction policies have had a similar goal of boosting the property tax base of the city by increasing the market for downtown commercial enterprises. Again such freeways have been constructed largely with state and federal funds.

The long-term effects of such policies on the welfare of the inner-city resident are not at all clear. Certainly, there has been limited accounting of the social benefits accruing from such policies. The short-term externality effects, however, are quite apparent. Both types of programs have required the clearance of residential areas which frequently house some of the poorest elements of the metropolitan population. Further, while both highway construction and urban renewal programs have required positive action in the areas of determining the availability of alternative housing prior to demolition and in providing relocation assistance, the history of such efforts is one of negligence; only more recently has the Department of Housing and Urban Development laid down more stringent guidelines for relocation policies to be pursued in urban renewal programs.

Urban renewal and highway construction programs, therefore, have often been accompanied by a net diminution in the amount of housing available to lower-income groups and to blacks in particular. The outcome has been the predictable one of overcrowding and/or increased rents for property of equivalent value.

Nor are the negative externalities imposed on the central-city poor as a result of such policies purely of the monetarily determinable type. Relocation often disrupts social relationships of great value to the lower-income person; the imposition of a freeway can have a similar effect.[23]

Housing Costs of Central-City, Lower-Income Groups: The differential ability of lower- and higher-income groups to select a suburban residence along with constraints on the expansion of lower-income housing in the suburbs should exercise a serious limitation on the supply of lower-income housing. This supply problem is aggravated by the effects of urban renewal and highway construction programs, as discussed above. One consequence of it should be that central-city, lower-income groups have to pay higher prices and rents for housing than they would if barriers to mobility and low-income housing expansion did not exist; such increased prices and rents would constitute yet another of the negative externalities resulting from movement barriers.

Further, movement barriers likely operate in both direct and indirect ways on the prices paid by low-income groups for housing of a given quality and quantity. With respect to indirect effects, for example, it is apparent that a slight easing of suburban zoning restrictions to permit middle- to lower-middle-income housing could have a useful impact on the prices of low-income housing in the central city. Much housing is occupied by low-income households as a result of a *filtering process*: low-income households tend to move into housing vacated by middle-income households. Yet, so long as zoning restrictions limit the expansion of middle-income housing in the suburbs, this filtering process will be arrested.

More directly, on the other hand, federally funded public housing for low-income citizens is currently confined largely to the expensive land of the central city. In New York City, for instance, it is estimated that it costs more than $30,000 per unit to build public housing. Terrace houses and garden apartments, on the other hand, could be built in the suburbs—zoning regulations permitting—for well below $20,00 per unit.[24] Yet, within the central city, the high price of public housing places clear lower limits on permissible rents and, therefore, on an expansion of low-income housing supply.

With respect to lower-income whites, the externality question has not been adequately researched. For blacks, however, there is evidence of negative externalities resulting from the barriers to movement created by discriminatory housing markets. In this context, not only is supply constrained but demand in many cities has expanded very rapidly largely as a result of the inmigration of Southern blacks. As a consequence, blacks face a more constrained housing market than whites in the same income

---

[23] Anthony Downs, "Uncompensated Nonconstruction Costs Which Urban Highways and Urban Renewal Impose Upon Residential Households," in Julius Margolis (ed.), *The Analysis of Public Output,* New York: National Bureau of Economic Research, 1970.
[24] Davidoff, Davidoff and Gold, op. cit.

bracket and often find themselves either: (1) paying the same rents as whites for housing which is inferior in quantity and quality, or (2) paying higher rents for accommodations of the same quantity and quality as that occupied by whites.

Concerning the first possibility, some 1960 Census data for Chicago are highly illuminating. In some census tracts, both white and black households paid median rents of $88 per month. The units rented by blacks were characteristically smaller, in worse condition, and more likely to be overcrowded than those occupied by whites. The median number of rooms rented by blacks was 3.35 compared with 3.95 for whites. Over 30 percent of the black units were dilapidated or deteriorating while this was true of only 11.6 percent of the white units. And, finally, 27.4 percent of the black units had over one person per room as opposed to 7.9 percent of the white units. Alternatively, blacks may occupy units of similar quality and quantity but pay higher rents. A study of low-income housing in Newark found that blacks consuming housing similar to that of whites paid rents which were from 8.1 percent to 16.8 percent higher.[25] A housing tax of a similar magnitude on blacks has been reported from Columbus, Ohio.[26] Given that blacks are usually of low income, excessively high rents force many blacks to pay a very high proportion of their total income for housing. This signifies that less money is available for other purposes, such as the purchase of a means of personal transportation.

Unfortunately, no comparable data exist for documenting the effects of movement barriers on the prices paid by central-city, lower-income whites. More adequately researched, though certainly not in the conclusive sense, is the issue of accessibility to employment. We can examine that particular negative spillover effect in somewhat greater detail.

Reduction in Access to Employment: To what extent has the changing locational pattern of employment opportunities within metropolitan areas imposed costs on central-city dwellers in the form of difficulties of obtaining employment and of holding on to jobs? The rationale for the hypothesized negative externality can be expounded briefly. Employment opportunities have been suburbanizing; central cities no longer have a monopoly on job opportunities and in some cases have experienced an absolute decline in employment. Lower-skilled jobs which can be speedily taught to workers with lower levels of education have tended to suburbanize fastest of all. The migration of middle- and upper-income households to the suburbs also has tended to alter the distribution of lower-skill jobs, such as domestic help and gardening. Meanwhile, the employment structure of the central city is increasingly dominated by white-collar jobs requiring high levels of education.

The changing locational pattern of employment has imposed minimal costs on middle- and higher-income groups and whites. They have been able to move to the suburbs to be close to their place of work or,

[25] D. M. Gordon (ed.), *Problems in Political Economy,* Lexington, Mass.: D.C. Heath, 1971, p. 370.
[26] Karen E. Walby, "Residential Segregation and Housing Prices," (Unpublished Master's Essay, Department of Geography, Ohio State University, March, 1971).

alternatively, they have access to an automobile, which gives them much greater discretion in their choice of residential location.

For lower-income whites and blacks, the suburbanization of employment has imposed substantial costs, since they have been able to adopt neither the personal mobility nor the residential relocation strategies. On the one hand, lower-income groups are restricted as a result of low levels of automobile ownership and the massive inadequacies of urban mass transit systems. In 1967, for those family units earning before tax incomes of between $2,000 and $2,999 only 53 percent owned an automobile. For families with income of between $1,000 and $1,999, the comparable figure was 38 percent, while for families earning below $1,000 a year only 25 percent owned automobiles.[27]

The deficiencies of urban mass transit systems add to these mobility problems. Largely as a result of increasing private automobile use on the part of the population as a whole and partly as a result of the increasingly dispersed demand for movement in geographical terms, there are few mass transit systems which do not find themselves in financial jeopardy. The dispersal of job opportunities to the suburbs away from their previous concentration in the central city has meant that a decreasing number of routes can sustain the demand necessary for a transit service to be profitable. Residential dispersion has had similar effects on mass transit system profitability.

Nor, on the other hand, have lower-income groups and blacks been able to adjust to the changing distribution of job opportunities by means of relocation. The barriers to movement (in the form of discriminatory zoning, dual housing markets, and high value properties) have tended to limit residential choice to the central city where job opportunities are declining either relatively or absolutely.

As a consequence of these difficulties, so the argument concludes, poor whites and blacks in central cities have restricted job choices compared to their more mobile and/or suburban counterparts. The lengthy and costly journey-to-work imposed by suburban jobs reduces the monetary return of a job compared with the monetary return from welfare payments. The mobility problem also makes job hunting and job holding more arduous. More sophisticated versions of this argument point to possible feedback effects which tend to reinforce this employment disadvantage. In particular, they point to the important role of personal communication in job markets, especially in lower-skill job markets and indicate that the fewer the number of central-city, lower-income individuals who hold jobs in suburban locations, the fewer the number of jobless who will hear about job opportunities there.

In summary, the major negative externality which seems to be at issue here is that imposed by independent suburbs as a result of their exclusionary residential policies. Such policies restrict the residential choices of central city, lower-income groups and their ability to adjust to

[27] John R. Meyer, and John F. Kain, "Interrelationships of Transportation and Poverty: Summary of Conference on Transportation and Poverty," *Conference on Poverty and Transportation: Report,* Brookline, Mass.: American Academy of Arts and Sciences, 1968.

the changing distribution of job opportunities. The resultant cost is borne by the individual in terms of unemployment and by the central city in terms of welfare payments.

This general argument relating job accessibility to poverty has proved highly persuasive with policy makers. As a result of this, the federal government has seen fit to subsidize all manner of demonstration and transit projects in major cities while at the same time devising policies to open up the suburbs residentially to lower-income, central-city groups.

There is, in fact, considerable circumstantial evidence which points up the mobility problems of the central-city poor and their relationships to unemployment. In many cities, for instance, we know that blacks have substantially longer journey-to-work trips than do whites. In Chicago, the average black work trip is 8 miles in length compared to 6 miles for whites.[28] Also there is no doubt that the mobility problem of the blacks lends itself to all types of extortion by unscrupulous entrepreneurs. In Los Angeles, transportation-cum-employment agencies have sprung up to recruit black maids and transport them to and from the middle-class suburbs where they work, charging the middle-class client $16 per day and paying the maid $10.

There are also some outstanding cases in which suburban relocation of employment has resulted in loss of jobs by those for whom mobility— either of the residential or journey-to-work variety—poses significant problems. When the National Bureau of Standards vacated its Washington location and moved to suburban Gaithersburg in Maryland, although total employment increased by 125, its black employment decreased by 75.[29]

Nevertheless, it is far from proven that central-city unemployment is a function of employment accessibility problems. It has been found in St. Louis, at least, that the relatively high rates of unemployment experienced by blacks in that city are more the result of frequent job changes than of inability to find employment.[30] Younger members of the black work force and those without dependents have been especially prone to job instability and unemployment. This has been attributed to the frustration of the low-paying jobs to which the black is confined both by job discrimination and skill limitations. The older and the less educated black worker is often more prepared to accept such jobs than is the younger and usually better educated black.

More recent research by Bennett Harrison lends a good deal of credence to this viewpoint.[31] With respect to sources of ghetto unemployment other than inaccessibility to jobs, Harrison focused on educational deficiencies. He found, however, that the marginal returns from increased education for blacks are extremely low compared with those for whites, despite the increased tendency of blacks to invest in their own education. In addition, no relationship was found between unemployment and

[28] *Time Magazine,* April 6, 1970, p. 48.
[29] Ibid., p. 53.
[30] Edward Kalachek and John M. Goering, "Transportation and Central City Unemployment": A Report Submitted to the U.S. Department of Housing and Urban Development, Washington, D.C., March, 1970, p. 8.
[31] Bennett Harrison, "Education and Underemployment in the Urban Ghetto" in D. M. Gordon (ed.) op. cit., pp. 181-190.

education for blacks whereas for whites increased education is associated with decreased unemployment.

In attempting to explain these findings, it was hypothesized that the combination of heightened job aspirations resulting from education and discrimination in the job market create job frustration among blacks. This generates reduced job attachment and a consequent cycle of job taking, job frustration, job leaving and unemployment accompanied by job search.

While ghetto unemployment can be conceivably ascribed to other sources, therefore, Harrison also presents evidence that accessibility to suburban job opportunities does not have a notable effect on job opportunities for blacks. While for whites such accessibility is associated with increased wages and reduced unemployment, such is not the case for blacks. In addition, the marginal returns from education for blacks are not significantly greater in the suburbs than in the central city. As Harrison states: "There is no evidence to support the widespread belief that through education, unskilled or semi-skilled nonwhite workers presently living in the ghetto can be 'suburbanized': relocated to the metropolitan ring, where their economic opportunities are assumed to be substantially greater."[32]

Clearly, if this analysis is correct then the "poverty and transportation" theory loses much of its force and the negative externalities attributed to suburban exclusionary policies are much diminished. The fact that there is evidence both for and against the "poverty and transportation" argument, however, suggests that we are some way from a definitive evaluation of those negative externalities. Indeed, much more research is required before we can provide an adequate empirical basis for policies aimed at mitigating central-city–suburban inequities of public provision.

In summary, however, it does appear likely that the costs imposed by such suburban movement constraints on central-city populations are not limited to the fiscal crisis brought about by the fiscal disparities problem. As middle-income relocation to the suburbs takes place and the fiscal position of the central city worsens, middle-income households remaining in the central city are able to obtain policies to their benefit rather than to the benefit of lower-income groups; *the threat of relocation to the suburbs* and elimination of the benefits which they provide for the central-city population as a whole *is* a potent one for central-city municipal governments. In addition, *urban renewal and highway construction policies* designed to lure middle-income households back either as residents or as consumers become necessary and impose costs on those of lower income in the form of relocation costs.

A third negative externality is in the form of *housing costs*. Constraints on locational choice for the lower income and black tend to increase the demand for the supply of appropriate housing and increase the rentals and sales values of such properties.

Finally, there is the "transportation and poverty" problem. Employment opportunities are increasingly suburbanized. Lower-income groups and particularly blacks, however, have great difficulty in securing housing

[32] Ibid., p. 189.

close to such job opportunities. These are the groups which are most likely to be lacking a means of personal transportation. The degree to which there is a relationship between *transportation and poverty*, however, has yet to be adequately substantiated.

While the forces leading to the residential arrangement of the metropolitan population should ultimately explain a great deal about the service-demand/tax-capacity ratio and, hence, about the geographical distribution of public provision, they are not the only factors which we need to consider. Also exercising an effect on demands for municipal services are more or less periodic movements into a municipality from outside it for purposes of work, leisure, etc. These movements are now considered.

INTRAMETROPOLITAN MOVEMENT AND THE ASYMMETRY OF NEGATIVE EXTERNALITIES

Temporary movements out of a municipality (such as the journey-to-work) impose costs on the jurisdiction through which they are directed and on the jurisdiction in which they terminate; expenditures on public safety, highway maintenance, and auto parking are clearly in demand here. Other movements are for the purpose of using recreational facilities which other municipalities have wholly or partly provided by means of a subsidy: parks and zoos, for example.

Within a metropolitan area, these negative externalities tend to be disproportionately imposed by independent suburbs upon the central city as a result of asymmetric movements of commuters and shoppers towards the central city and also because of the provision by the central city of recreational facilities which independent suburbs do not provide: subsidized art galleries, symphony orchestras, zoos, parks and municipal golf courses provide examples. This is often referred to as the "suburban exploitation of the central city" and, clearly, if verified, would serve only to aggravate the metropolitan fiscal disparities problem.

Much of the evidence for this effect relies on a study of central-city expenditures for 1940 carried out by the sociologist Amos Hawley.[33] Hawley focused on the seventy-six cities of 100,000 population or more and their surrounding metropolitan districts. Using data for these cities and their respective metropolitan districts, he computed a series of correlations between the public expenditures per capita of central cities, on the one hand, and various characteristics of the central city and of the remainder of the metropolitan area, respectively, on the other hand. These characteristics included such items as population size, labor force, white-collar labor force, and the number of houses. Hawley's rationale was that if there was a suburban exploitation of the central city, then correlations between central-city public expenditures per capita and characteristics of the surrounding metropolitan area would be higher than the correlations between those same central-city public expenditures per capita and the characteristics of the central city itself. In fact, the hypothesized relation-

[33] Amos Hawley, "Metropolitan Population and Municipal Government Expenditures in Central Cities," *Journal of Social Issues,* vol. 7, nos. 1 and 2, 1951, pp. 100-108.

ships seem to have been largely substantiated. While the population size of the central city explained only 15.8 percent of the variation in operating expenditures per capita for the central city, the population size of the surrounding metropolitan area explained over 31 percent of that same variation. Likewise, when all characteristics were considered in the form of a multiple correlation analysis, characteristics of the central city explained 43 percent of the variation in operating expenditures while characteristics of the surrounding metropolitan area explained a high 59 percent.

The common-sense plausibility of the exploitation argument, and such evidence as that of Hawley, have provided the basis for a number of central-city policies aimed at including suburban populations within the taxable population of the central city. The most important policies are: (1) a payroll tax on all individuals employed in the central city and (2) a municipal income tax levied not only on people who live in the central city but also upon those who work there.

In both Ohio and Pennsylvania, municipal income taxes are common and they are substantial assets as instruments of central-city tax policy. First, they carry considerable revenue clout. Although very few cities divide up the sources of the municipal income tax according to residents and nonresidents, some 1964 data for Cincinnati show that approximately 39 percent of the total revenues collected came from nonresidents.[34] The second advantage of the municipal income tax as a policy instrument is that it does not have the adverse effects on the location of business often associated with increased property taxes. Increased property taxes constitute an alternative assault on the metropolitan fiscal problem but they are often self-defeating since they lead to the suburbanization of business and a further decline in the central-city tax base. Taxation of employees does not involve the same risk.

Nevertheless, the case for suburban exploitation of the central city is far from proven and requires a much more detailed specification of the indirect costs and of the indirect benefits resulting from interjurisdictional movement than has been proven hitherto. At least two considerations show why there is room for legitimate doubt. First, while movements of commuters, shoppers, and recreators from independent suburbs to the central city do provide an added burden on the demand for public services, it is not true that they do not provide—indirectly at least—some countervailing addition to the tax base. Such movements are likely to involve, either as a direct or indirect product of the trip, the patronization of downtown businesses; this patronization will be reflected in the increased assessed value of the business property and an addition to the tax base of the city—and it is the patron who is indirectly paying the bill for property taxes on such business. Just as clearly, however, this does not take into account trips which are oriented toward services provided from nontaxable property. Such is the case of federal and state offices which

[34] Advisory Commission on Intergovernmental Relations, *The Commuter and the Municipal Income Tax,* Washington, D.C.: U.S. Government Printing Office, 1970, p. 9.

may occupy sizeable areas of the central city and reduce the city's tax base commensurately. In Detroit, 30 percent of developed land is lost to federal and state office buildings, schools and hospitals. This seems to be a particular problem for larger cities which contain a disproportionately large share of all federal and state building space and suggests that we do need a much more careful assessment of the costs and benefits of central-city–suburban movements.

A second reason for doubt is more dynamic in nature. Employment opportunities and retail opportunities are suburbanizing and, consequently, one would expect the asymmetry of commuter and shopper flows to be declining somewhat over time; one would anticipate, therefore, a greater equilibration in the mutual imposition of negative externalities by central city and suburb respectively. Asymmetry still exists but it is likely to decline over the longer term with important implications for metropolitan fiscal disparities.

Summary and Concluding Comments

Major inequities in public provision exist within American metropolitan areas between central city, on the one hand, and suburban municipalities, on the other. Generally, the central city has insufficient tax resources relative to the demands placed upon it for the provision of such public goods as education; however, suburban municipalities tend to have a high tax capacity relative to their burden of demands. As a consequence, not only may service needs be skimped in central cities, but property tax rates are also frequently higher. This problem of inequity is referred to as the "central-city–suburban fiscal disparities problem."

Nor are the dynamics of the problem reassuring. Relatively, the tax bases of the central cities are declining: this is largely a function of the suburbanization of businesses and of middle-class property owners. Relative decline is also apparent in the provision of services like education.

Factors contributing to the fiscal disparities problem arise at both national and metropolitan levels. A phenomenon of major significance has been and still is the migration to the larger SMSAs of poor, under-educated, and often unemployable individuals from the South and Appalachia, many of whom are black. This migration stream finds itself directed into the central cities of destination SMSAs, rather than into the suburban rings, and this has important implications for the level of demand for poverty-linked services and police protection, and for more income-elastic services such as education.

At the metropolitan level, clarification of the central-city–suburban fiscal disparities problem comes from constraints on residential and business location and from the patterns of daily movement between suburb and central city. For residents and business alike, the suburb provides a highly attractive location. The types of business and resident relocating to the suburb, however, are highly biased. Clean, nonpolluting businesses have been favored, while it is the white middle-class resident who, of all residents, has been able to relocate most easily into the suburbs. The reasons for these biases lie in certain constraints on the metropolitan property allocation mechanism: exclusionary zoning policies of suburbs, discriminatory housing markets, and high suburban property values.

While constraints on location exercise a considerable effect on the central-city–suburban fiscal disparities problem by filtering in the middle income and restricting the locational choice of the low income to the central city, they are by no means the only relevant factors within the metropolitan area. Also important are daily movements of the journey-to-work or shopping trip variety which tend to impose costs on the municipalities through which they are directed and on the municipality in which they terminate—for instance, expenditures on police, highway maintenance, and on public facilities such as zoos or symphony orchestras. Given the fact that until recently daily movements tended to be asymmetric with more movement by suburban residents to the central city than by central-city residents to the suburbs, it has been suggested that there is a *suburban exploitation of the central city.* To the extent that there is, this clearly imposes a further burden of demands on the central city relative to its tax capacity. Even with the elimination of metropolitan fragmentation, however, it is likely that there would be spatial biases in public allocation and consequent locational conflict. It is to those issues that we now turn.

CHAPTER 4

CONFLICT AND PUBLIC ALLOCATION WITHIN THE CITY

In the last chapter, we saw a substantial variation in environmental quality between the jurisdictions into which metropolitan areas are divided. Within jurisdictions, similar variations exist between neighborhoods. These variations, and the conflict resolution or public allocation process which generate them and which they in turn generate, form the focus of this chapter.

In the first half of the chapter, we attempt a characterization of the sources of those externalities which make neighborhoods variably attractive residentially. The outcomes of private and public investment decisions and the effect of public decisions on private decisions are our concern here. These decisions can be traced directly or indirectly to the public allocation process which mediates conflicts between localized populations that benefit to variable degrees from the externalities so created. In the second half of the chapter, the relationship between the public allocation process and neighborhood environmental quality is articulated.

The Private Component of Environmental Quality

The externality-producing activity of private resource allocation has important environmental effects. Substantial variations in environmental quality from one location to another, therefore, can be and are created by private investments within the city. Major environmental impacts of private investment within the city stem both from the location of investment in housing and the location of investment in health care facilities, retailing facilities, and employment opportunities. Generally, investment in private housing tends to be greater in middle-class and white neighborhoods of the city. Health care facilities, retailing facilities, and employment opportunities tend to be more accessible to those same localized populations.

Investment in housing includes investment in the maintenance, up-grading, and replacement of existing housing as well as investment in additions to existing stock; additions might be made on vacant lots or, alternatively, in the form of additions to existing buildings. Generally, between the different neighborhoods of a city there are great variations in levels of investment in the housing stock. At the polar extremes, however, we can recognize on the one hand the slum neighborhood and, on the other hand, the middle-class neighborhood.

In the slum neighborhood, housing is generally extremely dilapidated, testifying to low levels of maintenance. Abandonment of housing rather than its replacement is the rule. In New York City, for example 105,000 housing units (or enough to house the population of Newark) were abandoned between 1960 and 1969.[1] Public housing is also affected by abandonment—in St. Louis, only 17 of the 43 buildings of the giant Pruitt-Igoe housing project still have tenants.[2] Additions are rarely made to the housing stock of slum neighborhoods; rather, lots cleared of their existing housing stock are frequently allocated to such nonresidential uses as parking lots. The private investment which does occur tends to take the form of alterations to the physical fabric of buildings (partition walls, rewiring, etc.) which will permit more people to be squeezed into the existing space and increase the rate of return on an initially meager investment.

Middle-class neighborhoods, on the other hand, are characterized by extremely well-maintained housing in which existing housing at the end of its profitable life is cleared and replaced with new housing. In addition, where lots are available, additions to housing may be taking place.

These investment choices create a variety of externality effects which add to the environmental quality of middle-class neighborhoods and detract from that in lower-income neighborhoods. Some of the social costs of a poor housing environment are debatable. It has been argued, for example, that slums are breeders of crime, since overcrowding and lack of privacy generate a lack of respect for the individual. Other social costs of slums are fairly self-evident. For example, overcrowding and poor main-tenance make slum housing into fire traps. Also, slums are widely regarded as factors in the high disease rates characteristic of lower-income groups; over-crowding, inadequate sanitary facilities, and rodent control all con-tribute to this.

The location of investment in private housing tends to be paralleled by that of other private investments. Investment in health care facilities is an outstanding case in point. Within cities, major factors affecting the availability of physicians across census tracts appear to be income and race; comparing tracts, populations with higher median incomes tend to be served by greater numbers of physicians than populations having lower median incomes. Also, when allowance is made for this income effect, there is evidence that black tracts tend to be less well served than white

---

[1] *Newsweek Magazine,* February 28, 1972.
[2] Ibid.

tracts.[3] Physician services, therefore, tend to be least available in neighborhoods occupied by low-income, black populations.

Comparing poverty and nonpoverty areas in the city of Chicago, for instance, one finds that in 1965 there were twice as many physicians per thousand in the latter.[4] For ghetto and nonghetto populations, the disparity in physician availability is even greater. In the ghetto of southeast Los Angeles, for instance, there are 106 physicians for 252,000 people while in the surrounding county the ratio is three times greater.[5]

It is likely that differentials in physician availability do affect citizen investment in health care. This affects the likelihood of disease and the infection of others in the neighborhood. Low levels of personal investment in health care, therefore, do have important effects upon environmental quality; these low investment levels could conceivably be a result of low availability of physician services.

Certainly the incidence of contagious disease is comparatively high in big city ghettos. In 1960, for example, while the Watts ghetto in Los Angeles accounted for only 17 percent of the city population as a whole, it accounted for much higher percentages of the incidence of various diseases in the city. Sixty-five percent of all positive reactions to tuberculin skin tests in the city of Los Angeles occurred among Watts residents; Watts residents also accounted for 46 percent of the venereal disease, 45 percent of the dysentery, 43 percent of the rheumatic fever, etc.[6]

That accessibility to physician services probably plays an important role in this localized incidence of disease is suggested by two facts. First, blacks with incomes similar to those of whites spend less on medical services. Nonwhites with family incomes less than $2,000 were 12 percent less likely to have made a visit to a physician during the year than whites with similar family incomes. For nonwhites with family incomes of $10,000 or more, a visit was about 9 percent less likely than for a white with similar family income.[7] It will be recalled that for tracts of similar median income, physicians were less available in black tracts and this could account for reduced numbers of visits.

The second piece of evidence linking disease incidence to physician availability refers to levels of immunization. In ghetto populations, far lower proportions of children are immunized against diphtheria, whooping cough, tetanus, smallpox and polio. For example, Watts accounted for about 45 percent of all whooping cough outbreaks in the city of

[3] David Elesh and Paul T. Schollaert, "Race and Urban Medicine: Factors Affecting the Distribution of Physicians in Chicago," *Discussion Paper 99-71, Institute for Research on Poverty,* University of Wisconsin, Madison, Wisconsin, 1971.

[4] Joyce C. Lashof, "Medical Care in the Urban Center," *Annals of Internal Medicine,* vol. 68, no. 2, pp. 242-244.

[5] Fred J. Cook, "The Doomed of Watts," in David M. Gordon (ed.), *Problems in Political Economy: An Urban Perspective,* Lexington, Mass.: D.C. Heath, 1971, p. 321.

[6] Ibid.

[7] The National Advisory Commission on Civil Disorders, "Health in the Ghetto," in David M. Gordon, op. cit., p. 328.

Los Angeles.[8] Presumably, immunization could be more comprehensive if physicians were more accessible.

Private investments in housing, health care facilities, and other investments (such as those in retailing) are linked to a high degree by the market intended to consume the products of the investment. Investment in housing in poor neighborhoods is at low levels due to the difficulties of attracting upper-income residents who would be able to pay rents high enough to make the return on greater investment worthwhile. In those same neighborhoods, on the other hand, there is a demand for low quality housing on the part of people who can afford little more.

Investment in health care facilities exhibits a similar locational pattern for similar market-oriented reasons. Clients tend to patronize closer physicians rather than more distant physicians. In high-income neighborhoods, therefore, the physician can increase the price of an inelastic good, thereby increasing revenues.[9] In low-income neighborhoods, on the other hand, the demand for health care is more elastic and an increased price would likely result in reduced consumption.

Accessibility problems, of course, are considerably greater for the populations of poor neighborhoods. Low levels of automobile ownership inhibit access to physicians or retail facilities elsewhere in the city. The result is monopolistic exploitation by those retailers and physicians who do locate in the ghetto. A variety of evidence, for example, points to the limited geographical scope of shopping trip behavior by low-income residents as compared with those of higher income.[10] There seems little doubt that this immobility is a major reason for the low quality merchandise, high prices and extortionate credit practices to which the low-income consumer is subjected.[11] Similar documentation is required in such areas as physician and dental services, however.

The Public Component of Environmental Quality

While variations in private investment from one neighborhood to another create variations in environmental quality, public allocations are also instrumental in generating these differences. In this section we review locational variation in the allocation of: (1) public resources in general, (2) educational resources and (3) voting resources.

LOCATIONAL VARIATION IN PUBLIC RESOURCE ALLOCATION

Evidence of locational bias in the provision of a great number of municipal services is widespread. With respect to more mundane services, recent evidence emerging from a legal suit concerning the small city of Shaw, Louisiana is typical also of much larger cities in the U.S. The list of inequities is a depressing one. Almost 98 percent of houses fronting on unpaved streets in Shaw are black-occupied; 97 percent of the houses not

---

[8] Cook, op. cit., p. 321.

[9] Philip Lankford, "The Changing Location of Physicians," *Antipode,* vol. 3, no. 1, November, 1971, p. 69.

[10] David Caplovitz, *The Poor Pay More,* New York: Free Press of Glencoe, 1963. (See especially Chapter 4.)

[11] Caplovitz, op. cit. (See especially Chapters 2, 3, 6 and 7.)

Table 4.1. Summary of Responses to Questions Concerning Quality of Various Public Services.

	(a) Quality of public schools				(b) Parks and playgrounds for children			
	Negro		White		Negro		White	
	Men	Women	Men	Women	Men	Women	Men	Women
Generally satisfied	43	42	52	44	31	29	54	45
Somewhat dissatisfied	21	23	13	16	27	24	19	22
Very dissatisfied	15	14	9	9	26	28	18	18
Don't know	21	21	26	31	16	19	9	15
	100	100	100	100	100	100	100	100

	(c) Sports and recreation centers for teenagers				(d) Police protection			
	Negro		White		Negro		White	
	Men	Women	Men	Women	Men	Women	Men	Women
Generally satisfied	26	21	37	29	48	45	66	69
Somewhat dissatisfied	20	20	21	20	20	20	19	17
Very dissatisfied	31	29	22	20	27	25	12	9
Don't know	23	30	20	31	5	10	3	5
	100	100	100	100	100	100	100	100

	(e) Garbage collection			
	Negro		White	
	Men	Women	Men	Women
Generally satisfied	69	66	83	78
Somewhat dissatisfied	12	15	8	9
Very dissatisfied	15	16	7	9
Don't know	4	3	2	4
	100	100	100	100

Source: *Supplemental Studies for the National Advisory Commission on Civil Disorders,* Washington, D.C.: U.S. Government Printing Office, 1968, p. 40.

served by sanitary sewers are in black neighborhoods. All modern street lighting fixtures of the mercury vapor variety are confined to white neighborhoods of town and these white neighborhoods also have operational storm sewers and drainage ditches. Disparities between white and black neighborhoods also extend to the provision of fire hydrants, stop lights, and water main size.[12]

[12] Tom Wicker, "A Tale of Two Cities," *New York Times,* February 7, 1971.

Such disparities also are perceived to exist and they constitute an important source of conflict between the disadvantaged and the advantaged. Interesting, in this regard, is the survey of black and white experiences of city services made for the National Advisory Commission on Civil Disorders.[13] Table 4.1 summarizes black and white responses to a question concerning the quality of city services provided for their neighborhood; generally the question asked was, "First, I would like to ask how satisfied you are with some of the main services the city is supposed to provide for your neighborhood. What about the quality of the public schools (parks and playgrounds for children, etc.) in the neighborhood—are you generally satisfied, somewhat dissatisfied, or very dissatisfied?"

Table 4.2. Summary of Responses to Questions About Public Services Other Neighborhoods Receive.

	Negro			White		
	Men	Women	Total	Men	Women	Total
Better	12	9	11	17	19	18
About the same	59	62	60	66	64	65
Worse	22	21	21	7	8	7
Don't know	7	8	8	10	9	10
	100	100	100	100	100	100

Source: *Supplemental Studies for the National Advisory Commission on Civil Disorders*, Washington, D.C.: U.S. Government Printing Office, 1968, p. 40.

On every service considered, there is clearly greater dissatisfaction on the part of blacks than on the part of whites. The greatest black dissatisfaction is clearly in the area of police protection: as Table 4.1d indicates, blacks were over twice as likely to be dissatisfied as were whites.

A further question was asked concerning perceptions of discriminatory neighborhood treatment in the delivery of city services; the data defines a picture which is clearly as we might have anticipated. In response to the question, "Thinking about city services like schools, parks and garbage collection, do you think your neighborhood gets better, about the same, or worse service than most other parts of the city?", blacks were twice as likely to see their neighborhoods as obtaining service which was worse in quality (Table 4.2). Perceptions of discriminatory treatment are clearly important in the generation of conflict.

VARIATION IN EDUCATIONAL RESOURCE ALLOCATION BY GEOGRAPHIC LOCATION

In the last chapter we drew attention to the disparities which exist in educational provision between the suburbs and central cities of the

[13] Angus Campbell and Howard Schuman,"Racial Attitudes in Fifteen American Cities," Chapter 4 in *Supplemental Studies for the National Advisory Commission on Civil Disorders,* Washington, D.C.: U.S. Government Printing Office, 1968.

metropolitan areas. Such disparities were given a rationale largely in terms of the reliance of educational funding on local property taxes and, therefore, on the geography of assessed property value across school districts. That this explanation is not comprehensive with respect to all such geographical inequalities is confirmed by an examination of provision across schools within a district. Amazingly enough, disparities of a critical range exist at this level also, particularly within the central cities of metropolitan areas. Generally, children attending schools in the whiter and more middle-class areas of a school district tend to have more experienced teachers, to be taught in newer, more up-to-date buildings and to use the newest and least worn-out text books and equipment. Quite the reverse applies in the black and lower-class areas of the city—despite the greater need of pupils from those areas for educational services due to the lower educational investment provided by parents and friends. In addition, application of the neighborhood school principle in a residentially segregated environment results in disparities in exposure to middle-class peer environments, the importance of which has been identified by researchers such as Coleman.

The problem of interschool disparities, therefore can be discussed from three viewpoints: disparities in teacher quality, disparities in the capital equipment required by the education process, and disparities in access to middle-class peer groups.

There seems little doubt that, based on a variety of criteria, pupils at schools with more middle-class, white enrollments tend to get higher quality teachers than schools with more lower-class and/or black enrollments. This quality includes both the intellectual capacity of the teacher and teacher experience. Verbal skills, for example, are commonly regarded as a good index of IQ; by relating student social class to the verbal skills of their teachers it is possible to test for inequity resulting from the way in which teachers of quality are allocated or allocate themselves to schools. A study in the Detroit city school district disclosed that there was a very strong relationship between teacher verbal skill and student social class, since students of higher social class were being exposed to teachers of higher verbal skill and, therefore, presumably teachers of greater intellectual capacity.[14]

Disparities of a similar geographical incidence are also evident in data on teacher experience and qualification. A study carried out in Chicago in 1963 ranked public high schools by the socio-economic status of the population of surrounding neighborhoods and found that in the ten lowest ranking schools 36.8 percent of the teachers were not fully certified and the median teaching experience was 3.9 years. In contrast, in the ten highest ranking schools less than 1 percent of the teachers was not fully certified and the median teaching experience was 12.3 years. The

---

[14] James W. Guthrie, George B. Kleindorfer, Henry M. Levin and Robert T. Stout, "Educational Inequity, School Finance and a Plan for the '70's," in *Hearings Before the Select Committee on Equal Educational Opportunity of the United States Senate, 91st Congress, 2nd Session on Equal Educational Opportunity, Part 7—Inequality of Economic Resources,* 1970, p. 3458.

socio-economic contrast, of course, also corresponded with a racial contrast.[15] Similar relationships have been found in other cities.[16]

This disparity in experience and qualification is largely responsible for variations in per pupil expenditures across schools. Generally, pupils attending schools in poorer neighborhoods tend to have less spent on their education than do pupils attending schools in wealthier neighborhoods. More qualified and experienced teachers tend to command higher salaries, thus boosting expenditures at those middle-class schools to which they tend to gravitate. Further, there is good reason to believe that such disparities are not of minor significance in their impact on student achievement. Many empirical studies have verified a relationship between teacher experience and student performance on standardized achievement tests.[17]

Similar disparities exist with respect to the availability of the capital equipment necessary for education. These interschool disparities have been exhaustively documented for the elementary schools of the school district of a Northern central city and our discussion draws heavily on those findings.[18] Disparities were identified by differences in the treatment of four groups of schools, each group defined according to the average family income of the population of the school area; specifically the groups were defined as follows: Group I—$3,000-$4,999; Group II—$5,000-$6,999; Group III—$7,000-$8,999; Group IV—$9,000 and over. It was found that the schools in the lower-income groups—I and II—were considerably older than the schools in the upper income groups. The differences in mean age of school were: Group I—45 years; Group II—46 years; Group III—26 years; Group IV—25 years. On average, therefore, schools in poorer neighborhoods tended to be almost twice as old as schools in wealthier areas of the school district. These differences in age are clearly associated with deficiencies in the specific facilities available at schools in different types of neighborhood. Fifty percent of the Group I schools and 46 percent of the Group II schools lacked a science facility, for example, while less than 5 percent of the schools in more affluent neighborhoods in the same school district had such a deficiency. Similar disparities were apparent in the provision of conservatories and instrumental music and speech.

Such disparities clearly demand some type of equalization policy either by federal or state authorities. However, equalization policies have tended to be ineffective. Where federal funds do reach the more needy school districts, they often tend to be reallocated by local school district authorities in such a way as to benefit middle-class children as well as, or

[15] *Hearings Before the Select Committee on Equal Educational Opportunity of the United States Senate, 91st Congress, 2nd Session on Equal Educational Opportunity, Part 6—Racial Imbalance in Schools,* 1970, p. 3299.

[16] Patricia C. Sexton, *Education and Income,* New York: Viking Press, 1969, pp. 117-120.

[17] James W. Guthrie, George B. Kleindorfer, Henry M. Levin and Robert T. Stout, *Schools and Inequality,* Cambridge, Mass.: M.I.T. Press, 1971, pp. 79-84.

[18] Sexton, op. cit., pp. 123-132.

Fig. 4.1 Urban renewal and ghetto creation. Figure 1a (upper) refers to the residential pattern of blacks as it existed in the pseudonymous Iron City in 1950; Figure 1b (lower) describes that same residential pattern 12 years later. (Source: Theodore J. Lowi, "Apartheid, U.S.A.," *TRANS-action*, February, 1970.)

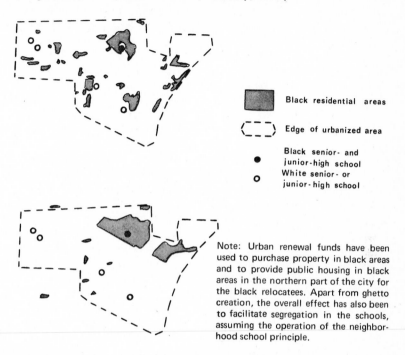

Black residential areas

Edge of urbanized area

Black senior- and junior-high school

White senior- or junior-high school

Note: Urban renewal funds have been used to purchase property in black areas and to provide public housing in black areas in the northern part of the city for the black relocatees. Apart from ghetto creation, the overall effect has also been to facilitate segregation in the schools, assuming the operation of the neighborhood school principle.

instead of, the poorer children for whom the aid was originally intended. The perverse reallocation of Elementary and Secondary Education Act Title I funds at the local level is well documented in this regard.[19]

Finally, with respect to peer environments, a variety of policies have as their end-product a reduction in the exposure of lower-class children to middle-class environments. For example, school location and pupil assignment policies may be used to maximize the white, middle-class nature of pupil enrollments at some schools and, consequently, maximize the black, lower-class pupil composition at other schools. With respect to pupil assignment, excellent examples have been unearthed in recent Congressional hearings on equality of educational opportunity.[20] In Pasadena, for example, there have been numerous cases in the past in which white middle-class students have been assigned to a more distant school with a predominantly white enrollment rather than to a closer school with a largely black enrollment.

[19] *Title I of ESEA: Is it Helping Poor Children?*, New York: NAACP Legal Defense and Education Fund, 1969.

[20] *Hearings Before the Select Committee... Part 6—Racial Imbalance in Schools*, op. cit.

More drastic policies with the same end may involve the relocation of residents under the auspices of urban renewal projects. This has been of some significance in the South where the typical black residential pattern has been a relatively scattered one. With legally enforced school segregation, such a residential pattern posed no threats for a maximization of peer group whiteness. The advent of court-ordered desegregation of schools, however, has presented difficulties for the white majority.

In a number of cities, this was foreseen and funds for urban renewal and accompanying relocation of residents used to implement a large scale reorganization of residential patterns. A case in point is provided by the pseudonymous Iron City discussed elsewhere by Lowi: Figure 4.1 presents the case rather graphically.[21] In 1950 (see Figure 4.1a) black residential areas were relatively scattered throughout the city; black school children attended the black junior and senior high school indicated. By 1962, however, the blacks had largely been relocated into the compact area in the north of Iron City indicated in Figure 4.1b. This relocation was facilitated by an urban renewal program which relocated blacks from their formerly scattered sites into public housing to form an incipient ghetto. Land vacated by blacks was then employed for white residential and business development. Most importantly, however, the neighborhood school principle would henceforth operate without disturbing the racial uniformity of school enrollments.

LOCATIONAL VARIATION IN VOTING RESOURCE ALLOCATION

A vote is a resource. Its value varies according to the degree to which it permits the voter to secure preferred policies. In addition, voting procedures are regulated by an institutional framework which can appreciably alter that value from one neighborhood to another. Alteration by such means is particularly feasible where preferences for public policy are spatially clustered. Gerrymandering, of course, is a widely recognized method of altering the value of a vote from one area to another.

These facts are very apparent in manipulation of the institutional framework to minimize the policy value of the votes cast by residents of black neighborhoods. Consider, for example, the effects of the municipal electoral system on the representation of black neighborhoods in a city. Generally, one is impressed by the inability of black voters to elect blacks to city councils in proportion to their representation in urban electorates. Usually, only in cities with smaller black proportions has parity been attained. It is clear, however, that there is a relationship between the attainment of parity and the municipal electoral system. On the one hand, in nonpartisan, at-large elections, the black candidates must (without the benefit of a party label) face the whole, predominantly white, electorate. In such circumstances, the support of newspapers and civic associations is vital and blacks, therefore, have difficulty obtaining representation. In fact, based on a regression analysis of data for twelve cities, it would appear that the relationship in cities with nonpartisan, at-large electoral

---

[21] Theodore Lowi, "Apartheid U.S.A.," *TRANS-action*, February 1970. Reprinted in Michael N. Danielson (ed.), *Metropolitan Politics*, Boston: Little, Brown and Company, 1971, pp. 340-352.

Fig. 4.2 Black population and black council representation for cities with non-partisan, at-large electoral systems. Generally, the black share of city council power tends to decline as the fraction of the population which is black increases. (Source: Lee Sloan, " 'Good Government' and the Politics of Race," *Social Problems*, vol. 17, no. 2, Fall, 1969, Table 1, p. 163.)

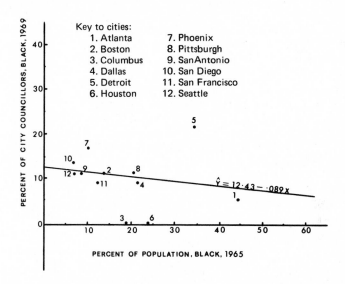

systems is quite perverse (see Figure 4.2); there is a slight negative relationship wherein cities with larger black proportions have lower proportions of city council seats held by blacks. Quite apart from this quantitative handicap, however, the blacks elected under such a system will often be conservative on those very issues which affect the perverse spatial allocation of public goods simply because they must be acceptable to the largely white electorate.

In the partisan ward system, on the other hand, the chances of a black neighborhood electing a black representative are much greater. As Figure 4.3 shows, the relationship between the proportion of city council seats held by blacks and the proportion of the population which is black is positive and almost approaches parity; parity would be achieved in this case with a regression coefficient of 1.0 whereas it happens to be .84.

The divergent implications of different municipal electoral systems for the representation of blacks suggest the quite clear possibility of manipulation of that system to the advantage of the white majority. The plausibility of such action is suggested by a case study carried out in Lakeland, a city of approximately 85,000 close to Detroit.[22] Prior to 1962, the electoral system was of the ward type. Highly pertinent to our argument, however, is the fact that one of the wards was 90 percent black and had been in the habit of electing a highly militant black to the city

[22] Lee Sloan, " 'Good Government' and the Politics of Race," *Social Problems*, vol. 17, no. 2, Fall, 1969, pp. 161-175.

council. In 1962, however, there was a move to change the electoral system to an at-large system. It is significant that the petitions for a referendum on the proposed charter amendment to change the electoral system were circulated by members of the Junior Chamber of Commerce with the support of the local newspaper. Further, the newspaper made it quite clear in its support that the aim of the operation was to eliminate the election of militants such as the black representative. The resultant voting in the referendum closely followed racial lines with whites in favor of the change and blacks opposed. Considerable evidence, therefore, exists for the thesis of purposeful adoption of the at-large electoral system to limit the quantity and to control the quality of black representation.

Fig. 4.3 Black population and black council representation for cities with partisan, ward electoral systems. Generally, the black share of council power tends to increase as the fraction of the population which is black increases. The proportionality effect is also fairly equitable so that the black proportional share of council in a given city is approximately the same as the black proportion of the population as a whole. Comparison with Figure 4.2 suggests that this greater equity may be related to the electoral system. (Source: Lee Sloan, " 'Good Government' and the Politics of Race," *Social Problems*, vol. 17, no. 2, Fall, 1969, Table 1, p. 163.)

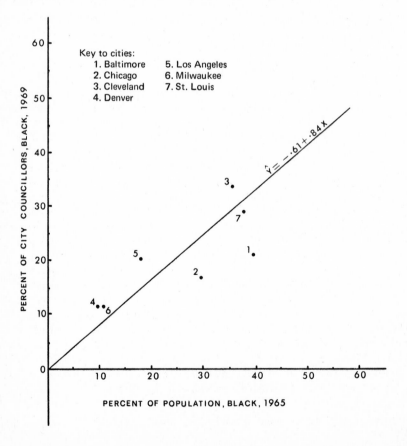

The Public Component of Environmental Quality and Private Investment Decisions

Clearly, public policies have strong effects upon the environmental quality of different neighborhoods within the city. At the same time, they create opportunities for private investment in those same neighborhoods. These opportunities have varying rates of return attached to them. It is possible, therefore, to envisage a process in which private investment choices generate an intensification of differences in environmental quality resulting directly from public policy.

This process is particularly apparent in the housing market. A variety of public policies with neighborhood bias have affected investment in the maintenance and improvement of housing. These have ranged from urban renewal to the location of schools. Generally, they have worked to the benefit of middle-class groups and whites and to the detriment of lower-class groups and blacks.

The dynamics of neighborhood change envisaged by these remarks can be discussed with reference to two polar types of neighborhood change: *gentrification* and *deterioration*. Deterioration needs little further explanation. It is a process in which public and private investment in a neighborhood decline concurrently and middle-income groups are replaced by lower-income groups. Gentrification, on the other hand, is a term frequently used in the British real estate industry; it refers to a process in which private investment in a neighborhood increases markedly and in which lower-class residents are displaced by middle-income residents. It is usually accompanied by increased public investment in the neighborhood. Gentrification will be discussed first. We will then examine the reverse process of deterioration and conclude the section with some summary comments on processes of neighborhood change.

GENTRIFICATION

Public policies may induce gentrification in a variety of ways. For example, public policy may *inadvertently* make a neighborhood more attractive to middle-class residents: a park may be laid out or through traffic may decline with the construction of a parallel freeway. The neighborhood becomes more attractive to live in and property values increase. Property developers purchase properties and convert them to middle-income use by investment in external and internal refurbishment. As middle-income residents move in, the values of adjacent properties rise. This provides incentives for landlords to evict low-income tenants who cannot afford the increased rents and sell out to a property developer. Conversion to middle-income use by refurbishment will then take place until a compact block of properties has been so transformed.

In other cases, gentrification has been an *intended* objective of public policy. This has been particularly apparent in the use of federal urban renewal funds by local urban renewal agencies. Since 1951, a major aim of urban renewal has been the rehabilitation of old houses with a view to eliminating the problem of relocation consequent to demolition. However, federal loan programs have been insufficiently generous to permit low-income occupants to upgrade their properties to the quality prescribed by such a rehabilitation program; the result has been a selling out of property to the more affluent who can afford the requisite rehabilitation. Gentrification under such auspices has occurred in a number of lower-class areas containing old housing of some architectural merit and appealing to the middlebrow. Notable in this respect are such middle-class areas as Georgetown (Washington, D.C.), Society Hill (Philadelphia), and German Village (Columbus, Ohio).

Gentrification, therefore, involves government provision of externalities which increase the rate of return from private investment in housing. On the one hand, the externalities may result from public facilities such as parks or quiet streets. On the other hand, the externalities may result from a government guarantee of middle-class neighbors able to provide public behavior and status externalities. Designation of a relatively large area for rehabilitation with urban renewal funds can provide this guarantee. It can be strengthened further by a judicious choice of area so that it will be effectively insulated from surrounding neighborhoods by busy highways, rivers, freeways, etc.

In the process of gentrification, however, there is a mutuality in the relationships between private investment and externality-providing public policy. Public policy induces private investment while private investment generates pressure for public provision. Generally, as investment in an immobile resource increases, the benefits from localized public provision increase. An important consequence in areas undergoing gentrification, therefore, is the emergence of residents' associations. These lobby for increased externality-generating public provision in the neighborhood.

A good example of this process is provided by the recent emergence of a middle-class enclave in the Barnsbury district of the largely working-class Islington area of London.[23] Attracted by the accessibility of the area to the center of the city and by the possibilities of renovation, professional families in the late 1950s and early 1960s started buying and refurbishing for their own use cheap, run-down Victorian houses which had previously been divided into apartments. The increasingly middle-class character of the area led to an increase in property values such that: (a) lower-income families were discouraged from moving into the area, and (b) property developers put pressure on working-class tenants of the rent controlled houses and apartments in order to persuade them to leave. Pressure took a variety of forms ranging from small money transactions to physical intimidation.

Since then, the middle-class families of the area have organized themselves to obtain public policies providing localized externalities which could make the area more attractive and, incidentally, as a result of rising property values, increase the middle-class homogeneity of the area. Organization has taken the form of a pressure group—the Barnsbury Association—and representation on the Islington council. The major public good realized by this collective action has been the introduction of

[23] Peter Kellner, "One-Way Scheme for a Revolt," *London Sunday Times,* January 10, 1971.

a traffic scheme to make the area residentially more attractive. "No Entry" signs, roadblocks, and one-way streets have been introduced with an eye to deterring the use of local streets and parking space by nonlocals, and therefore, to increasing local property values.

DETERIORATION

Public policy also can operate in the reverse direction: the provision of facilities haivng negative externalities such as street widening, failure to maintain zoning and housing code provisions, and the threat of urban renewal. All these can induce a decline in property values, an unfavorable environment for private investment in housing and conversion for use by low-income groups who are prepared to live in low-quality housing. The consequent syndrome of physical deterioration and social change then ensues.

Of particular significance in neighborhood deterioration are changes in student composition at local schools. Composition in terms of both social class and race is important. There is, for example, the widely held middle-class view that lower-class students from educationally deprived backgrounds will retard the intellectual development of their middle-class peers. There is also the real problem of interracial hostility and violence between white and black students. As a consequence, the siting of new schools and the funding of old schools to enhance their attractiveness for middle-class residents become important. These efforts are rather clearly exemplified by the attempts of the Bagley Community Council in northwest Detroit in the early 1960s. The objective of the council was to maintain residential attractiveness through increasing the attractiveness of the offerings made by the public school system.[24] These policies took a number of forms, some of them successful and some of them not.

There were attempts, for example, to encourage educational innovation in local schools. Efforts were made to provide foreign languages instruction at the Bagley elementary school. Related to this and also to the ethnic composition issue were efforts to decentralize the program for accelerated learners offered by the city-wide Cass Technical High School. Decentralization of this program boosted the holding power of threatened neighborhoods such as Bagley by permitting the local high school to offer the program and concurrently an element of within-school racial segregation due to the fact that accelerated learners' classes consisted largely of white pupils.

As with gentrification there is mutuality in the relationships between externality-providing public policy and private investment. While changes in public policy induce decreases in investment by private individuals in a neighborhood, so those same changes in private activity generate, directly or indirectly, public withdrawal of positive externalities. As private investment diminishes, property values decline and the social composition of the area changes, so for a variety of reasons public provision will deteriorate. Teachers, for example, develop an increasing aversion to

[24] Eleanor P. Wolf and Charles N. Lebeaux, *Change and Renewal in an Urban Community,* New York: Praeger, 1969, Chapter 3.

teaching in schools which are becoming increasingly black in their pupil composition and request assignments elsewhere; the more effective teachers are likely to wield considerable bargaining power with the school system and obtain such reassignment. Likewise, as white households are replaced by less affluent black households, the local Parent-Teacher Association will suffer a decline in participation and therefore in its bargaining power relative to the city school system.

In addition to a deterioration in the provision of such public services as education, the application of existing laws designed to coordinate private investment in a socially beneficial manner also is likely to suffer. This is very clear in the notable differences in adherence to housing code provisions between low-income and middle-income neighborhoods. Housing codes are designed to place a lower limit on maintenance expenditures so as to diminish the negative externalities imposed on neighbors consequent to undermaintenance. In low-income neighborhoods, however, adherence to housing codes by landlords is frequently dependent upon tenant pressure and such pressure is unlikely for a number of reasons.[25]

For a start, most residents in such areas have extremely low levels of information about housing code provisions. For many, urban life is a novelty so that the idea of publicly enforced housing standards is quite new. In addition, the housing they occupy may appear satisfactory when compared with the standards to which they have been accustomed in their original rural environment.

Where residents do have information, on the other hand, they may lack information about alternative residential opportunities to make their demands for improved housing effective. More common still is restriction of low-income housing choice for institutional reasons. Dual housing markets and exclusionary zoning restrictions on an expansion in the supply of low-income housing serve to limit residential opportunities and reduce the bargaining power of tenants.

For reasons of an institutional and knowledge nature, therefore, there is a strong, highly inelastic demand for low-quality housing in those localized areas of the city where the restricted residential alternatives of low-income groups are located. As a consequence, the political contest between owner and tenant over adherence to housing codes has been an unequal one.

SOME SUMMARY COMMENTS ON NEIGHBORHOOD CHANGE

In summary, one is impressed by two features of the investment processes underlying change in neighborhood quality. First, there is their strongly *cumulative nature*. Public investments create a favorable environment for private investments. These private investments create a favorable environment for further private investments which stimulate in turn further public investments. Reduced private investment, on the other hand, will stimulate neighborhood change leading to a reduction in the investments

---

[25] This discussion relies heavily on Jerome Rothenberg, *Economic Evaluation of Urban Renewal*, Washington, D.C.: The Brookings Institution, 1967, pp. 43-46.

of others; public agencies permit a deterioration of the neighborhood infrastructure while insurance companies withdraw their protection from those who are prepared to invest in the deteriorating neighborhood.

Once initiated, therefore, gentrification and deterioration are difficult to arrest. Negative externalities induce more allocations which produce additional negative externalities. In the neighborhood undergoing gentrification, on the other hand, positive externalities, whether privately or publicly provided, generate further allocations having positive externality effects. The result of these strong *positive feedback processes* of gentrification and deterioration is that neighborhoods are much more variable with respect to environmental quality than if allocation responded less to externality considerations. Public policy aimed at reducing such neighborhood variations, therefore, clearly needs to manipulate the availability of those goods generating externalities for private investors and biasing their decisions.

Second, however, the force of these positive feedback effects is very dependent on the *atomized nature of the private investment decisions creating externalities.* The dependence of the private investor upon the allocations of his neighbors, for example, or upon the vagaries of public provision is partly a function of deficient capital assets. Increased capital assets would permit the locator either to (a) purchase the property rights of individuals owning properties in the neighborhood or (b) obtain adherence to public provisions—such as housing codes—regarding the use of that surrounding property.

Large corporate institutions, therefore, do have the capital assets to pursue locational strategies of a strictly private nature. They have the power, consequently, to preserve or alter the quality of their environment and can be less dependent on the private investment decisions of others in the neighborhood or on localized public provision. Universities are an important case in point.

In a number of cities, such as Philadelphia, New York, Chicago, and Cleveland, the neighborhoods adjacent to universities have often deteriorated to the point at which they constitute a threat to the continued existence of the institutions. Increasing levels of neighborhood crime, for instance, deter both students and faculty from taking up residence in the immediate area and constitute a threat not only to recruiting but also to the effective functioning of the university. In addition, universities have been expanding and in this context surrounding neighborhoods pose a different type of threat: land users consuming land that would otherwise be available for expansion.

An excellent example of this is provided by the activities of the University of Chicago in the deteriorating area surrounding it. Through its political arm (the Southeast Chicago Commission) appointed for this purpose, the university has been able to encourage faculty, staff, and student residence in the area both by buying up property for such purposes and also by extending mortgages to those willing to buy homes in the area.

A specific instance of the way in which the university was able to use its power to thwart threats to the neighborhood is provided by the use made of its wide contacts with insurance and banking companies in Chicago. The Southeast Chicago Commission was aware, for example, that a local hotel was being used for various illegal purposes; information collected by two private policemen hired for the purpose was forwarded to the company insuring the hotel. The insurance company disclaimed all knowledge of the activity and cancelled its coverage. Without insurance coverage, the hotel's mortgage holder demanded immediate repayment of the loan, resulting in foreclosure, a change in proprietorship, and elimination of the activity.[26]

More recently, in Nashville, Vanderbilt University has invested appreciable sums of money in purchasing property in a surrounding white middle-class area.[27] Purchase has been spatially scattered and the properties so purchased demolished or alternatively allowed to stand vacant and deteriorate. The objective has been a systematic engineering of negative externality effects for the remaining residents of the area to induce a decline in their maintenance investments and a deterioration of environmental quality to that point at which the area could be declared fit for urban renewal. The properties then could be acquired by the Nashville Housing Authority, cleared of structures and repurchased at a federally subsidized price for redevelopment by the university.

Even in these cases involving large capital assets available for purposes of engineering neighborhood stability or change, the property owners also have evinced considerable interest in securing publicly-provided positive externalities for the area. In both the Chicago and Vanderbilt instances, for example, the universities have lobbied for urban renewal in their immediate vicinity. This has been partly due to the federal subsidy for purchase of property for redevelopment. More importantly, however, it probably derives from the problems of strategic bargaining encountered in large-scale land assembly.[28] Clearly, there are limits to the ability of locators with large capital assets to secure the immediate neighborhood— limits which can only be surmounted by public policies providing localized benefits. It is to the public allocation process responsible for such policies that we now turn.

The Public Allocation Mechanism

It is clear, therefore, that there are substantial differences in environmental quality from one city neighborhood to another. Some of these differences are the direct result of public allocation; still others are created by private investment seeking out opportunities produced in a locationally variable manner by the public allocation process.

In addition, differences in environmental quality between neighborhoods stimulate conflicts between those same neighborhoods or are

[26] Peter Rossi and Robert A. Dentler, *The Politics of Urban Renewal*, New York: Free Press, 1961, pp. 82-83.

[27] *Newsweek Magazine*, October 11, 1971, p. 105.

[28] See, for example, Otto A. Davis and Andrew Whinston, "Economic Problems in Urban Renewal," in E. S. Phelps (ed.), *Private Wants and Public Needs*, New York: W. W. Norton, 1965, pp. 145-146.

themselves the results of a conflict resolution process. Parent-Teacher Associations contest with one another for the scarce educational funds available to a school district. Neighborhood associations compete to attract money for street and curb maintenance or to keep away the freeway or urban renewal.

We come logically, therefore, to the question of why the competing demands of neighborhoods for what the political system has to offer are arbitrated in the way they are. Alternatively, why is it that some neighborhoods get more of the positive externalities and fewer of the negative externalities? To answer these questions some conceptualization of the public allocation process is needed.[29]

A CONCEPTUALIZATION

Initially we assume a government and an electorate of voters who elect the government and to whom the government, therefore, is responsible. The government's interest is in providing those policies which will ensure its continued tenure of office, i.e., the government maximizes its own utility. As Downs has written elsewhere: "In effect it [the government] is an entrepreneur selling policies for votes rather than for money."[30] The individual elector's interest, on the other hand, is in securing those policies which will maximize his utility. The policies at issue have either explicit or implicit locational effects. The government's problem in a geographical context, therefore, becomes one of satisfying localized populations containing sufficient electors to ensure its continued existence. The elector's problem, on the other hand, is to secure policies which provide his neighborhood and, therefore, him and his private property with positive externalities.

Of critical significance to understanding those public allocations important to the environmental quality of neighborhoods and resulting from the interaction of government and elector, is *the information problem.* Governments need information on the needs of the electorate: in brief, what public policies are desired? Electors, on the other hand, need to provide this information if they are to secure the desired positive externalities for their neighborhood. We have, therefore, two resource allocation problems. On the one hand, the government must allocate resources to securing information about different public needs: to which public needs should it attend? The elector, on the other hand, must decide how much to allocate to the provision of information to the government relative to his other demands. Each is considered in turn.

---

[29] This conceptualization is based on the general approach of Anthony Downs. See Anthony Downs, *An Economic Theory of Democracy,* New York: Harper Row, 1957, and an article summarizing some of his more relevant ideas, "An Economic Theory of Political Action in a Democracy," *Journal of Political Economy,* vol. 65, no. 2, April, 1957, pp. 135-150. Also useful has been Jerome Rothenberg, "A Model of Economic and Political Decision Making," in Julius Margolis (ed.), *The Public Economy of Urban Communities,* Washington, D.C.: Resources for the Future, 1965.

[30] Downs, "An Economic Theory of Political Action...," op. cit., p. 137.

THE OPTIMAL GOVERNMENT ALLOCATION OF RESOURCES TO INFORMATION ACQUISITION

In order to maximize utility, governments must provide policies which satisfy elector needs and which satisfy to the extent of ensuring the government's continuing tenure of office. The information acquired must refer to: (1) *the nature of the need to be satisfied*; for example, the need to reduce traffic congestion along a particular street or the need to allocate more money to a particular school; (2) *the effects of satisfying that need upon government utility*: what are the costs and benefits of a policy designed to satisfy a need upon support for the government? If funds are reallocated from middle- to lower-class neighborhood schools, what effect will this have on the election campaign funds of the government or the desire of its supporters to continue to live in the jurisdiction?

Clearly, there is an allocation problem. The government does not have infinite resources to allocate to the identification of needs and to the evaluation of them from the viewpoint of its own utility. Given the infinity of citizen demands about which the government might obtain information, how should it allocate resources across those needs? Briefly, a utility-maximizing government will allocate resources to secure information about a need to the point at which the net benefits to itself from securing the information are maximized. Information provides benefit to the government in the form of a policy which increases the probability of continuing tenure of office. Information, however, is not cost-free. The cost must be balanced against the benefits which the government derives from a literally more informed policy.

This has important consequences. Where *zero-cost* information is supplied to the government about a specific need, more information will be acquired by the government about that need than about needs for which zero-cost information is not supplied. Consequently, lobbying and "squeaking wheels" become of large significance in policy-making. "The squeaking wheel get the grease" is as true of localized populations as it is of individual electors.

In brief, the amount of information which the government acquires about a certain need and about the costs and benefits to itself attached to satisfying that need is very dependent on how much information is received.

THE OPTIMAL CITIZEN ALLOCATION OF RESOURCES TO INFORMATION PROVISION

The elector's interest is in providing information that will induce policy-generating benefits for his neighborhood. For maximum effectiveness, the citizen must convey information not only about the nature of his needs but also about his terms of trade with the government: what utility can he provide the government in return for a desired policy?

This information can be provided in a number of ways: voting, writing to legislators, petitions, threats, demonstrations, civil disobedience, and letter-writing campaigns. For each individual elector, each form of information provision is theoretically comparable in terms of a common-utility scale measuring the *cost of information provision and the benefit from information provision.* We assume here, therefore, the existence of a unit of information. Whatever the mode chosen for providing that information, a unit has the same cost and the same effect on policy as any other unit of information. Clearly, changes in investment in information provision will involve changes in the mode of provision. The act of voting is a low-cost form of information provision; participation in organized activities such as letter-writing and demonstrations, on the other hand, is much more costly.

The basic problem confronted by the citizen is how much of the scarce resources at his disposal should he invest in information provision? Assuming utility maximizing and omniscient resource allocators, he will *allocate resources to information provision to that point at which net benefits from the government policies induced are maximized.* In order to develop this idea theoretically, it assumes that we can define: (a) an information provision benefit curve and (b) an information provision cost curve such that net benefits are maximized where the vertical distance between the two curves is maximized. We assume that units of information provided are measured along the horizontal axis; the costs and benefits of information provision are measured along the vertical axis. The problem, theoretically, therefore, reduces to one of identifying the factors affecting the forms of those curves. We assume throughout that the aim is to secure policies conferring localized benefits in the form of positive externalities.

The Benefits from Information Provision. For a given level of information provision, the benefits for the elector from allocating resources to such provision will be greater: (1) the greater his investment in immobile resources the return from which is dependent upon public provision, and (2) the greater his investment in mobile resources the return from which is dependent on public provision in the neighborhood rather than elsewhere. Each is considered briefly.

Investment in Immobile Resources: Information provision by the elector affects the provision of neighborhood externalities which affect, as we have seen, the rate of return from private investments. All other things being equal, those who have invested in mobile resources are relatively indifferent; if the externalities are provided in other neighborhoods, relocation without loss is feasible. On the other hand, for those whose investment is in immobile resources, the rate of return may be highly contingent upon public provision in the neighborhood.

Within the city, buildings and capital equipment are the most important of the immobile resources at issue. In central cities, for example, banks, retail stores, and insurance companies have very large investments, the rate of return from which is threatened by those forces which are moving wealth and population to the suburbs. As a consequence, these private interests have been importantly represented in attempts to regenerate the commercial and residential attractiveness of the central city by means of publicly-provided externalities.

Investment in Mobile Resources: Many resources are mobile, but returns to investment in those resources may be highly variant locationally. Often the rate of return to a mobile resource is higher within the neighborhood than elsewhere. Assuming that maximization of the return to private investment is contingent upon public provision, the expected benefits from local positive externalities are increased. Consequently, the expected benefits from a given investment in information provision are also increased.

Blacks form a group for whom returns to private investment are locationally very different. Provision of externalities within their neighborhood permits blacks to receive higher rates of return on their investment than does provision elsewhere. Consider black investment in labor skills, for example. Given barriers to black residence, the rate of return outside of the ghetto is very dependent upon commuting costs. Provision of employment opportunities in the suburbs, therefore, can greatly reduce the investment yield for that group. For whites, on the other hand, locational variation in rates of return to investment in mobile resources is much diminished.

The Opportunity Costs of Information Provision. Information, however, is not cost free; there is an opportunity cost. Resources are used, the values of which are computable in terms of the utility deriving from allocation of those same resources to alternative uses. Three major considerations affect the opportunity costs confronted by an individual citizen: (1) the supply curves for the factors employed in providing a given amount of information, (2) the individual's utility function specifying the value to him of alternative uses of the resources employed in securing those factors, and (3) income: this, along with the price ratio, defines the specific consumption possibilities curve for the individual on his utility-mapping.

Supply Curves: In order to provide information, a variety of resources are required. These resources involve outlays which could be allocated to other activities. Some of the more important resources include bargaining resources, infrastructural resources, and manpower resources.

Bargaining resources may be readily available, in which case they are infinitely cheap; or, they may not be available at all, in which case, they are infinitely expensive. Of major significance as a bargaining resource is control of other resources providing large positive externalities for the government. Threatened uses of this control in a bargaining situation can include varying degrees of withdrawal of those externalities. The private economy, for example, controls sources of campaign funds for the government; in addition, it controls employment levels. It is a relatively cheap strategy for the industry concerned to claim increasing unprofitability and the possibility of unemployment if cost-imposing legislation passes into law. Clearly, the value of such bargaining resources is contingent on other facets of the employment structure; these include the degree to which the employer in question controls the fortunes of the urban labor force. In one-industry or in one-company towns this can be very large. Consequently, steel companies have found it easy to counter any threatened pollution control measures in such single-industry towns as Youngstown and Duluth.

Other forms of information provision require an investment in *infrastructure*. Usually individual resource allocators within an economy are incapable of threatening disutility for the government sufficient to induce a desired policy. By joining with others in an organization lobbying for such policies, however, a threat of much greater disutility can be conveyed. The benefits accruing to the organization then take the form of a public good equally available to all members. An organization, for example, provides an instrument for discovering the extent and intensity of like-mindedness of people on an issue; it provides a forum for information exchange, a means of coordinating individual gripes, and of articulating demands in an attention-grabbing manner.

Organization, however, requires a fixed investment in the creation of communication lines both within the organization and with other corporate bodies; it also requires the creation of a constitution to arbitrate the demands of members, and the generation and maintenance of interest in the activities of the organization (in some cases, the latter may require a full-time secretariat). Such costs are large and often pose an insurmountable threshold for individual households in impacted neighborhoods. They are reduced substantially, however, where corporate bodies with localized clienteles (such as churches and neighborhood improvement associations) are already in existence.

Third, *manpower resources* are required in order to develop an effective counterstrategy to the agency of threat to the neighborhood. Arguments for the location of facilities having negative externality effects, for example, can be countered by a variety of legal, urban planning, or economic arguments. This presupposes access to these types of knowledge. For an organization, therefore, lawyers and urban planners can be highly important members. Without their services, often donated, legal services and planning consultation may have to be purchased.

It is clear that these resources can be substituted for one another to some degree depending on their relative prices at a particular time. If an individual has control of allocations providing large positive externalities for the government, organization and investment in infrastructure and manpower resources may be unnecessary. Alternatively, the possession of bargaining resources of value in intercorporate bargaining may reduce infrastructure costs. Due to their control of advertising revenues, for example, businessmen may be able to exercise a significant depressive effect on the infrastructural cost of maintaining communication with the electorate at large via the mass media.

Utility Functions: The value of the resources expended in these ways, however, depends very much on the individual's *utility function*. Particular interest here concerns the degree to which the demand for information provision relative to other demands is income-elastic. It seems likely, for example, that information provision is valued more relative to other goods by the wealthy than by the poor. There is no doubt, for example, that wealth is correlated with organizational membership.[31] Within a city, higher-income groups generally belong to appreciably more voluntary organizations than lower-income groups. In addition, rates of participation in political activities are also greater for higher-income groups: they vote more, they are more likely to belong to political parties and to be officers in such parties, and to hold legislative office, for example, than lower-income individuals.[32]

Income: Whatever the form of the utility function, however, it seems safe to assume that information provision has a positive income elasticity. An increase in income leads to a displacement of the consumption-possibilities line on the utility surface. An increase in income, therefore, permits increased purchases of those resources employed in information provision without a commensurately greater increase in opportunity costs. Consequently, all other things being equal, one would expect the opportunity cost curve of information provision to be of an appreciably reduced slope for those with access to greater capital assets.

DEVIATIONS FROM OPTIMAL INVESTMENT IN INFORMATION PROVISION

Once benefit curves and opportunity cost curves for information provision are defined for individuals, it would be a relatively simple matter to identify optimal levels of information provision, i.e., for a specific individual, the optimum level is that at which the difference between benefits and opportunity cost is maximized. In the real world, however, optima have the habit of not being achieved. Two sources of deviation are: (1) market imperfections resulting from inadequate knowledge and (2) market failure. These need to be considered prior to the characterization of the major features of urban power structure.

Information. Information about policies affecting neighborhood welfare is not equally distributed across different social groups. If a neighborhood is threatened in some way by an impending negative externality, action to counter the threat is obviously dependent upon having information about it and about those responsible for it. Also, it is important that such information be acquired early. For example, when plans are well advanced for a freeway or a municipal stadium, the agency of threat such as a municipal planning authority has a considerable investment at stake: properties may have been purchased prior to demolition, for instance, and considerable expense incurred in hiring private planning consultants. Deflecting the threatening land use elsewhere, therefore, will involve a

[31] Morris Axelrod, "Urban Structure and Social Participation," *American Sociological Review,* vol. 2, February, 1956, pp. 14-18.

[32] See, for instance, Lester Milbrath, *Political Participation,* Chicago: Rand McNally, 1965.

commensurately large investment of resources in information provision by local individuals.

Conversely, it is apparent that considerable implementation advantages will accrue to those agencies of threat which can proceed with a minimum dispersion of information to the impacted neighborhood and, if the neighborhood does obtain an inkling, a maximum dispersion of uncertainty. Of major relevance in this context is the concept of *purposeful ambiguity*.[33] This involves the purposeful use of ambiguity by the agency of threat in negotiations in order to gain an advantage. It may take a number of forms.

On the one hand, for example, there may be purposeful misinformation and a public posture of vagueness, making it difficult for the impacted neighborhood to identify the agency of threat with which to negotiate. On the other hand, the agency of threat may make concessions to the neighborhood which are later ignored or modified so as to be no longer acceptable; the effect of such a strategy is to increase the belief of the impacted population in the sincerity of the negotiator during earlier phases of the implementation process and, therefore, to allow the agency of threat to increase its investment in the neighborhood and maximize its negotiating power.

An excellent example of such purposeful ambiguity is provided by the negotiations concerning the final route plan for Interstate 40 through Nashville, Tennessee.[34] The route selected was regarded as destroying a great deal of black business and residential property as well as cutting through the campuses of three major black educational institutions including Fisk University and Tennessee A & I. Black opposition to the plan, however, was successfully countered by a strategy of purposeful ambiguity exercised by the proponents of the plan. Both misinformation and ultimately worthless concessions were apparent in this strategy.

It is evident that the planners were able to keep secret much information about the highway and its impact upon the ghetto of North Nashville. In May 1958, when the route plan had assumed final form, a public hearing as specified by law was scheduled. However, information concerning the meeting was posted only in areas *outside* the black community and was inaccurate as to the date of the meeting. On other occasions, deputations of black citizens were fobbed off with the claim that no final route had yet been selected and that it was still in the planning process. The effect of such misinformation and vagueness was to frustrate and bewilder the impacted population rather than to lead to the unambiguous identification of a source of threat with which to negotiate. Nothing tangible against which to protest was revealed.

[33] John Seley and Julian Wolpert, "A Strategy of Ambiguity in Locational Conflicts," in Kevin R. Cox and David R. Reynolds (eds.), *Locational Approaches to Power and Conflict,* Beverly Hills: Sage Publications, Inc. (forthcoming), 1973.

[34] John E. Seley, "Spatial Bias: The Kink in Nashville's I-40," *Research on Conflict in Locational Decisions,* Regional Science Department, University of Pennsylvania, Philadelphia, Pa., Discussion Paper No. 3.

Likewise, the planning authorities at later stages of the controversy did make concessions on actual physical changes in roadway design and also promised a degree of citizen participation in the planning process. These never materialized, but they did serve to enhance general citizen belief in the desire of the government to be just.

While examples such as this are suggestive as to the distribution of information across different neighborhood groups, however, they are far from conclusive. Not much is known about the distribution of community knowledge. What little is known tends to support the contention that upper- and middle-income groups have advantages.[35] This is partly due to habits of newspaper and magazine readership. Probably much more important, however, are the contacts which middle- and upper-income groups enjoy with those responsible for, or who know of, threats to neighborhoods: government employees, realtors, city councillors, etc. Further, middle- and upper-income groups with their higher levels of formal education are likely to be much more knowledgeable about the machinery of the governmental and planning process so that they are in an advantageous position to seek out more information about public provision regarding their neighborhood.

Market Failure. Investment in information provision to induce policies favorable to the individual's neighborhood has benefits not confined to the individual making the investment. Consequently, as we saw in Chapter One, it is in everybody's interest to let someone else make the investment and provide the positive externality. The logical consequences of universal adoption of this decision calculus is that no one invests, i.e., there is market failure. This is often referred to as the *free rider* problem.

More recent literature, however, has concentrated upon forces which make the emergence of the free rider problem more or less likely. A major force underlying the free rider phenomenon is the failure to perceive interdependence. Provision of the public good or externality is dependent on individuals perceiving a relationship between *joint* participation with others and provision of the good. Where individuals, for whatever reason, fail to see the relevance of their participation for the achievement of desired levels of provision the free rider problem emerges. This perception of interdependence seems to be critically related to group size.[36]

Perceptions of interdependence and, henceforth, investment in information provision are more likely in smaller groups of individuals preferring a particular policy. In a small group, the individual's *fractional contribution* to the achievement of the desired level of provision is very evident. His failure to contribute would have a noticeable impact upon the level of provision. In larger groups, on the other hand, the individual's fractional contribution is extremely small. His failure alone, therefore, to contribute would have an imperceptible effect on provision levels. In such groups, it

[35] Gresham M. Sykes, "The Differential Distribution of Community Knowledge," *Social Forces*, vol. 29, May, 1951, pp. 376-382.
[36] For an exposition of this viewpoint see: Mancur Olson, *The Logic of Collective Action*, Cambridge, Mass.: Harvard University Press, 1965. For a simpler exposition see: Robert L. Bish, *The Public Economy of Metropolitan Areas*, Chicago: Markham, 1971, pp. 30-34.

is difficult to develop a conception of interdependence. The consequence is that larger groups tend to suffer from the *free rider* problem to a disproportionate degree. Small groups, on the other hand, such as groups of businessmen, are much more likely to invest in information provision within the urban political system than are larger groups.

Urban Power Structures

We have been attempting to identify the major forces affecting the decision to invest in the provision of information to the government. Clearly, those who invest more are more likely to secure the policies which they demand than are those who invest less. The approach, therefore, affords us a means of specifying those groups of resource allocators who characteristically determine urban policy, i.e., the components of the urban power structure. At the same time, and more importantly, it allows a specification of those locales within the city for which public policy externalities are demanded. In this way, we may be able to offer some explanation for differences in environmental quality between neighborhoods within the city.

Briefly, two major groups appear to dominate the allocation of public resources in favor of their localized investments in the city: the downtown business elite and middle-class householders. Each group is considered in turn from the viewpoint of policies demanded and from the viewpoint of the factors affecting investment in information provision.

THE DOWNTOWN BUSINESS ELITE

This consists of the owners—or their representatives—of large commercial properties in the downtown area and of ancillary activities. In the former category, therefore, are the boards of insurance companies, department stores, and banks with mortgages extended to other central-city property owners. In the latter category fall the newspapers which rely heavily on central-city business fortunes for the sustenance of their advertising revenue.

The major policies for which this group lobbies are those that will sustain and increase the business vitality of the central city. As the suburbs have become more attractive for commercial activity, increased investment has been required in these information provision efforts. A number of policies proposed, therefore, are designed to retain central-business district accessibility to the labor force and to the more affluent consumer. Freeway construction, mass transit, and urban renewal for middle-income housing all have been urged on this basis. Still other policies involve increased public investment in the central business district itself: subsidized convention centers and subsidies to theaters provide examples of this type of policy.[37] The additional interest of the downtown business elite in low property tax assessments needs no further explanation.

---

[37] On the situation in San Francisco, for example, see Danny Beagle, Al Haber, and David Wellman, "Creative Capitalism and Urban Redevelopment," in David M. Gordon (ed.), op. cit., pp. 400-404.

Major factors explaining the high level of lobbying activity conducted by the downtown business elite include the *immobility of their investments* and the ready availability to them of *bargaining resources.* Downtown commercial buildings represent large capital investments which depreciate in value slowly. Suburbanization of business, consumer markets, and labor forces pose a clear threat to the rate of return from these capital investments.

Adding to the immobility of such investments are legal restrictions on business mobility. Under many state laws, central-city banks are prohibited from opening branches at will in the suburbs; many public utilities with large investments in the central city are prohibited from extending their franchises into suburban areas.

While the benefits to be gained from a given investment in information provision are relatively large, the cost of such provision may be relatively minor as a result of the availability of bargaining resources. Not only do central-city business interests contribute a large amount of revenue directly to the city treasurer's office, they also make important contributions to the city's economic health in the form of employment. As a result of control of these positive externalities, it is cheap and plausible to threaten a scaling down of business activity unless certain policies are pursued. In this respect, there is a growing and more or less persuasive mythology concerning the effects of urban policy on revenue generation. It is widely known, for example, that increased business taxes in New York City stimulated a scaling down of business activity until the taxes were lowered.[38]

However, these are not the only reasons why we would expect the interests of the downtown business elite to be assiduously protected and advanced. For instance, a well-maintained and financed *organizational infrastructure* in the form of a Chamber of Commerce usually is available to press the interests of members. The *small size* of the business elite likewise facilitates the development of new ad hoc organizations for new purposes. In addition, individual businesses have the *capital assets* to invest at low opportunity cost in the purchase of specialized legal and planning advice. Most large businesses, for example, have their own legal staffs trained in the relevant locational issues likely to affect business fortunes. In a recent book on public policy in Oakland, Edward Hayes has admirably documented the role of downtown business interests in promoting urban renewal in that city and the cost factors working in favor of such groups.[39]

MIDDLE-CLASS HOUSEHOLDERS

A variety of evidence points to greater investment in information provision by middle-class households, in order to secure public provision

---

[38] On this point see Dick Netzer, "Federal, State and Local Finance in a Metropolitan Context," in Harvey S. Perloff and Lowdon Wingo (eds.), *Issues in Urban Economics,* Washington, D.C.: Resources for the Future, 1968, p. 445.

[39] Edward C. Hayes, *Power Structure and Urban Policy: Who Rules in Oakland?*, New York: McGraw-Hill, 1972.

of positive externalities and enhance the residential attractiveness of their neighborhoods. A variety of neighborhood actions are reported in local newspapers: the contesting of applications for zoning variances, petitions for a local stop light or against street widening, etc. Scrutiny of the neighborhoods involved ususally reveals them to be middle income in residential composition.

In addition, participation in voluntary organizations having localistic ends is greater in middle-income neighborhoods. Schools in middle-class areas have Parent-Teacher Associations which are much more strongly supported than those in lower-class or black areas. In the study reported on earlier,[40] it was found that in elementary schools in areas with the highest economic status (Group 1), the ratio of students to members of the Parent-Teacher Association was 100:74. In Group 4 schools—in the lowest income neighborhoods—the corresponding ratio was 100:10.

Middle-class residents, therefore, invest appreciable amounts of time and money in attempting to enhance the residential quality of their neighborhoods. This involves both attracting the propitious and keeping away the obnoxious. Parent-Teacher Associations lobby for increased expenditures in the local schools, for example, or for a redrawing of the neighborhood served by a particular school. Other organizations monitor changes likely to pose threats to the neighborhood and mount campaigns of opposition when necessary.[41]

The major reason for the greater activity levels characteristic of middle-income residents is their *investment in an immobile resource—residential property*—the return from which is dependent upon public provision of positive externalities. Middle-class neighborhoods are owner-occupied neighborhods. Threats to the neighborhood, such as racial invasions or a high density housing development on an adjacent tract, are therefore evaluated from the viewpoint of their impact on property values. In a recent survey of middle-class reaction to low- and moderate-income neighbors, the major reason given for opposition was that property values would fall.[42]

Lower-class neighborhoods, on the other hand, have only low levels of owner occupancy; the typical resident has little in the form of investment in immobile resources to protect therefore. The landlords assume a crucial role in such areas and their major concern is with maximizing the cash return on their investments. Toward these ends, apartment owner associations have been a significant source of opposition to public housing policies which might increase the supply of low-income housing and erode the market for deteriorating neighborhoods.[43]

---

[40] Sexton, op. cit.

[41] An excellent description and analysis of such lobbying activity in a middle-class neighborhood threatened with racial invasion is contained in Wolf and Lebeaux, op. cit., Part 1.

[42] Gruen, Gruen and Associates, "Directions for the Suburbs," in *Hearings Before the Select Committee on Equal Educational Opportunity of the United States Senate, 92nd Congress, First Session on Equal Educational Opportunity, Part 21—Metropolitan Aspects of Educational Inequality,* 1971, p. 10557.

[43] For the case of Oakland, see Hayes, op. cit., Chapter 4.

A variety of evidence supports this view of the crucial role of property ownership. Consider, in this regard, the reaction of the largely working-class Brookline-Elm community of Cambridge, Massachusetts to the impending location of a freeway—the Innerbelt—in their community.[44] Homeowners were a minority in the area, forming only 23 percent of the sample studied, but they showed significantly greater interest in collective action to oppose the freeway. While a majority of the homeowners attempted to ally themselves with a protest organization which had developed elsewhere in the path of the proposed freeway, only 30 percent of the renters did so.

In addition, middle-income neighborhoods within the city have a powerful bargaining resource. They supply disproportionately large fractions of city revenue in the form of property taxes and, in some cities, municipal income taxes. Current images probably exaggerate the magnitude of this contribution to fiscal surplus, but it is an image which can be exploited by middle-income households. Therefore, the threat of relocation for central-city councils and school boards is a potent one; it probably accounts in some degree for footdragging over school busing to achieve racial integration of schools and for underassessment of middle-income residential properties for property tax purposes.[45]

Information provision by middle-income households also is facilitated by the relatively low cost with which essential resources can be procured. Many middle-income neighborhoods, for example, have *infrastructural advantages* in the form of permanent residents associations or taxpayers associations designed to monitor impending or current locational change and lobby when necessary. An advantage of such organization is that levels of information are likely to be much higher. Many organizations, for example, have a roster of members who take turns to peruse the columns of the local newspapers for announcements of public hearings regarding zoning variances, etc.

The necessary *manpower resources* also are likely to be cheaper. Effective lobbying frequently requires legal and planning knowledge and advice. Lawyers and planners are much more likely to be represented in the middle-income neighborhood than in the lower-income neighborhood and to be interested in enhancing it.

A final consideration is that of *communication resources*. In order to be effective, information concerning neighborhood needs and its implications for government utility must be delivered to those ultimately responsible for policy. This is greatly facilitated by common membership in organizations and common residence. Those directly active in party politics and government also are likely to belong to a variety of voluntary organizations in the city as a whole: the Chamber of Commerce, the real estate

[44] Gordon Fellman and Roger Rosenblatt, "The Social Costs of an Urban Highway: Cambridge and the Inner Belt Road," in *Conference on Transportation and Poverty: Report*, Brookline, Mass.: American Academy of Arts and Sciences, 1968.

[45] For locationally biased assessment policies in Boston, see David E. Black, "The Nature and Extent of Effective Property Tax Variation Within the City of Boston," *National Tax Journal*, vol. 25, no. 2, June, 1972.

board, the Freemasons, the symphony orchestra society, charity, and community action organizations. It is known that participation in these organizations is strongly correlated with income.[46] The organizations, therefore, provide a medium for contact and communication between middle-income residents and those responsible for those public decisions enhancing or detracting from neighborhood quality.

In addition, due to their middle-income status, policy makers share residential neighborhoods with other middle-income residents. Therefore, they are readily accessible through a variety of neighborhood associational links and activities to the lobbying of their immediate neighbors. School boards, for example, are dominantly composed of middle-income people. A variety of studies have demonstrated that approximately 75 percent of all school board members are business proprietors or managers, professionals, or wives of such men; from 3 percent to 15 percent of board members are manual workers.[47] Nor is this of trivial significance. School boards exercise final authority in school matters; they appoint the superintendent, for instance, and he hires teachers. One should not be surprised, therefore, at the variety of policies designed to conserve the advantages which schools in middle-income neighborhoods already have.[48]

A notable exception to the low levels of investment in information provision characteristic of low-income neighborhoods has been recent lobbying by black groups in order to improve ghetto environmental quality. Generally, lobbying has been on behalf of such policies as community control of schools, community economic development and increased employment opportunities, urban renewal involving low-income housing for ghetto residents, housing code enforcement, etc.

A specific case exemplifies this activity: a locational dispute generated by the impending location of a medical school in Newark. The original threat to the Newark ghetto community came from the decision of the Jersey City Medical Center to accept an invitation from Newark and relocate there on land to be cleared for urban renewal purposes and also on land previously set aside for lower-income housing. In response to this threat, two local black organizations emerged: The Newark Area Planning Association, which sought legal assistance from the NAACP, and the Committee Against Negro and Puerto Rican Removal, which attempted to directly influence the involved Departments of Health, Education and Welfare (HEW) and Housing and Urban Development (HUD).

HUD and HEW were in particularly crucial positions as far as the purse strings controlling redevelopment were concerned. On the one hand, HEW was responsible for half the funding of the Medical Center; on the other

---

[46] Axelrod, op. cit.

[47] Robert J. Havighurst, "Knowledge of Class Status Can Make a Difference," *Progressive Education,* vol. 27, no. 4, February, 1950.

[48] One attempt to develop such a relationship can be found in William Bunge, et al., "A Report to the Parents of Detroit on School Decentralization," in Paul W. English and Robert C. Mayfield (eds.), *Man, Space and Environment,* New York: Oxford University Press, 1972, pp. 514-517.

hand, HUD was concerned that its funding for urban renewal be contingent on adherence to national urban renewal goals, particularly those specifying that priority should be given to projects providing low- and moderate-income housing and employment for local residents. With prodding from the NAACP, the Committee Against Negro and Puerto Rican Removal, and from the Newark ghetto riots of July 1967, HEW and HUD submitted to the local planning authority in Newark joint criteria for funding the Medical Center and specifying community involvement, construction employment for local residents, relocation plans for residents, and the training of neighborhood residents in health fields.[49]

These specifications provided the basis for negotiations between the ghetto pressure groups referred to above, the Medical Center, and the Newark Housing Authority. Major features of the solution arrived at included provisions allowing for minority group representation in construction and employment of neighborhood residents by the Medical Center when completed.

With this example in mind, consider reasons for ghetto lobbying of this nature. Blacks, like whites, invest in resources such as job training and residential property from which they expect a payoff. For blacks, however, unlike whites, *the rate of return is likely to be much lower in locations outside the ghetto.* This is a direct result of obstacles to black residential mobility.[50] The rate of return to investment in job search and job training in the suburbs is reduced by the heavy commuting costs necessitated by barriers to black purchase of suburban residential property. The rate of return to the investment of resources in housing is likewise vitiated by the restriction of black choice to "changing areas" in which public investments in schools, roads, parks, etc., will be run down. Consequently, the benefits to be obtained from public policies of "gilding" the ghetto are considerably greater for ghetto residents than if they had a greater degree of residential discretion.

Further, ghetto populations are obtaining *bargaining resources.* An important effect of the ghetto riots of the 1960s was to increase the bargaining power of blacks. For city governments, riots provide only negative externalities in the form of deterioration in the city business climate and a flight of white middle-class residents who provide the ultimate base of support for the government anyway. It is significant, therefore, that the New Jersey Medical Center controversy which was settled by means of considerable concessions to blacks was widely regarded as a major factor in the Newark ghetto riots at that time. It is also apparent that many blacks regard riots as useful bargaining resources.

---

[49] A lengthy description of the Medical Center controversy is provided in Leonard J. Duhl and Nancy J. Steetle, "Newark: Community or Chaos," in Leonard J. Duhl (ed.), *A Symposium on the Urban Crisis,* Berkeley: Center for Planning and Development Research, University of California, 1968, pp. 408-445.
[50] This interpretation is also suggested by Julius Margolis, "Decentralization and Urban Programs," in Anthony H. Pascal (ed.), *Thinking About Cities,* Belmont, Calif.: Dickenson Publishing Company, 1970, pp. 60-61.

A variety of survey evidence indicates that in the past blacks have expected riots to induce public concessions for ghetto neighborhoods.[51]

Third, and finally, there is an emerging *national organizational infrastructure* which lowers the costs of political action for blacks. Of particular importance in this regard is the NAACP which can make available organizational, legal, and planning resources to local ghetto organizations. A considerable body of federal legislation has recently expanded the rights of ghetto residents appreciably; changing administrative guidelines for policy application have also tended to favor the same groups. The *organizational infrastructure* provided by the NAACP provides a continual monitoring of these changes and a medium for making that knowledge available to local ghetto groups.

Summary and Concluding Comments

Clearly, there are substantial variations in environmental quality between neighborhoods within cities and particularly within central cities. Some of these variations can be traced to private investment patterns: for example, patterns of investment in housing and in health care facilities. Other components of that variation can be attributed to decisions made in the public allocation process: for example, decisions regarding the allocation of educational resources across neighborhood schools. Thirdly, much can also be attributed to the interaction of decisions in both the private and public sectors of urban resource allocation; we emphasized this interaction in our discussion of the polar processes of neighborhood change—deterioration and gentrification.

Given the public nature of many of the forces generating this pattern, it can be interpreted in two ways which are sequentially complementary. On the one hand, neighborhood inequalities can be regarded as the outcome of a process of resolution of conflict between localized populations: for instance, between the ghetto and the middle-class neighborhood. Alternatively, the pattern of locational inequity can be regarded as a major force generating further locational conflict—the demands of ghetto populations for community control of schools in order to rectify some of the imbalance in resource allocation, for instance; and the opposition to busing from middle-class neighborhoods in order to protect the privileges of their schools.

Great significance in understanding these inequities and the resolution of the conflicts which they generate, therefore, attaches to the public allocation process in the city. The welfare of localized populations is very dependent upon provision by urban government of positive externalities which not only provide direct benefits, but also indirect benefits in the form of an increased return to private investment. Provision of these externalities, however, depends on the provision of information: informa-

---

[51] This is exemplified in T. M. Tomlinson and David O. Sears, "Negro Attitudes Toward the Riot," Chapter 7 in Nathan Cohen (ed.), *The Los Angeles Riot*, New York: Praeger, 1970. See also Campbell and Schuman, loc. cit., p. 49.

tion about the positive externalities required and the utility accruing to the government from providing those externalities.

Investment in information provision is clearly something which varies among electors. Logically, we would expect those for whom the net benefits of information provision are greater to invest more in such provision. This assumes that we can evaluate opportunity cost and benefit curves for electors. Benefit curves are affected by such factors as the immobility of resources, the rate of return from which will be strongly affected by localized public provision. Opportunity cost curves are affected by such considerations as the supply curves for the necessary resources.

Although these hypothetical curves determine optimal elector invest-ments in information provision, some deviations can be expected. On the one hand, variations in the information which electors have about policies likely to, or capable of, affecting them introduce some imperfections into the market. On the other hand, the public good nature of policies resulting from information provision can result in market failure.

These considerations, however, help us to understand the major components of urban power structures; they emerge as groups of electors for whom net benefits from information provision are large: the down-town business elite and middle-class residents. Both have investments in immobile resources: the first in downtown business property, the rate of return from which has tended to decline as a result of suburbanization of markets, labor forces, and other business; the second from residential property. Both also have infrastructural resources and bargaining resources in the form of positive externalities for the city government, the withdrawal of which can be threatened.

As in the case of interjurisdictional inequalities in environmental quality, however, the inequities existing at the neighborhood level are a continuing source of conflict; present controversies regarding busing and urban renewal are cases in point. We come logically, therefore, to a consideration of policies capable of resolving these conflicts in a socially more satisfactory manner than the urban public allocation process has yet been able to. This forms the focus of our final chapter.

CHAPTER 5

POLICY IMPLICATIONS

The message emanating from the topics discussed in this volume and relevant to policy makers is simple and unequivocal—public provision within the American city is riven with inequity with respect to groups defined both in social and in locational terms. On the one hand, it is clear that middle- and upper-income neighborhoods of the city tend to get more of what is given publicly than do the lower-income and black areas. This has been particularly apparent in the areas of education and police protection, though it is also apparent in such functional areas as garbage collection, highway maintenance, street lighting, and the location of obnoxious facilities. On the other hand, the social differences tend to be exacerbated by locational considerations independent of social class; the populations of independent suburbs tend to get a more attractive public goods package than do those remaining in the central city. This provides central-city, middle-class populations with important leverage—in the form of the threat of relocation—in obtaining public provision concessions from their hard-pressed municipality.

As far as the social correlates of this inequity are concerned, there is obviously a correlation with inequity in private income. The privately wealthy tend to be the ones benefitting most from municipal tax and expenditure policies while the poor gain least. As Harvey has noted elsewhere, such inequities in public provision detract from the income redistribution effects of a progressive federal income tax on private individuals and permit the wealthy to gain further private income advantages: consider, for instance, the property value advantages resulting from a favored status with respect to public provision.[1]

---

[1] David W. Harvey, "Social Processes, Spatial Form and the Redistribution of Real Income in an Urban System," in M. Chisholm, A. Frey and P. Haggett (eds.), *Regional Forecasting*, London: Butterworth, 1971.

Public policies aimed at producing greater equity in public allocation across subareas of the metropolis are prompted by two major considerations. First, there is the moral one: the immorality of permitting public opulence to coexist with public deprivation—and often in defiance of all legal prescriptions and proscriptions. And second, there is the efficiency argument. Policies which result in inequity tend ultimately to be inefficient from the standpoint of the total welfare of society. Production of goods and services does not attain the level which it would in the absence of such inequity, for example. There is, therefore, a sizeable literature on the economic gains to be made by society from greater educational provision for blacks, economic gains which would in their turn permit a far more substantial funding of education than is possible at present.[2] Not only that, but it is apparent that the despairs and thwarted hopes generated by inequity are counterproductive. Riots clearly reduce the productive efficiency of society; and while the links between *individual* deprivation and rioting are far from apparent, it is also unlikely that rioting would have occurred under circumstances of more equitable public provision.

Formulation of effective policies designed to eliminate the social injustices which plague the American city, however, presupposes some knowledge of the factors producing that allocation in the first place. Summarizing a great deal of the material which has gone before, it appears that two major and related items have to be considered here, one of them explicitly locational in character and the other quite clearly social in character. First, there is the *spatial organization of the urban political system.* What is received publicly depends very much on location relative to such spatial artifacts of a political system as job opportunities, schools, freeways, and the boundaries of different municipalities and of school catchment areas. Residence on one side of a municipal boundary may mean that the average school pupil benefits from educational expenditures, say, $100 per year greater than those received by the average pupil on the other side of the boundary. Within the same municipality even, residence in a given school catchment area can bring a child into contact with a much more opulently endowed teaching system than residence in a neighboring school area. The same general significance of location can be applied to the impact of other localized features of the urban political system such as freeways, one-way streets, and crime protection.

Second, there is *the allocation of private resources across individuals within the urban political system.* On the one hand, there is the largely white middle class; on the other hand, there is the lower class with its sizeable black component. The distribution of private resources is important from at least two points of view. First, income differences tend to be strongly associated with investment in lobbying action. The middle class

---

[2] See, for instance, Walter W. Heller, "Economics of the 'Race Problem' " in *Hearings Before the Select Committee on Equal Educational Opportunity of the United States Senate, 91st Congress, 2nd Session on Equal Educational Opportunity, Part 7—Inequality of Economic Resources,* 1970, pp. 3644-3651.

and the white, therefore, are likely to attempt and to be successful in, for instance, gerrymandering school districts to maximize the middle-class/white character of the school districts in which they reside, altering the electoral system to dilute the quantity and quality of ghetto representation, and deflecting the obnoxious from their neighborhoods.

Furthermore, private resources appear to be an important correlate of externality provision and, therefore, of locational acceptability. Consequently, the residents of the middle-income suburb accept only the white middle-class resident with his desirable public behavior and ability to purchase high assessed value properties and exclude the lower class and the black by discriminatory zoning and real estate practices. As a consequence, the lower class is excluded from benefitting from the large investments which such suburbs characteristically make in education and from the new employment opportunities which they have been increasingly monopolizing.

In conclusion, two types of policy seem called for: (1) changes in the spatial organization of the political system and (2) changes in the distribution of private resources. Amelioration of the urban crisis could be effected by either type of change or a combination of such changes; this is apparent in the policies frequently proposed. Here we initially consider changes in spatial organization and then discuss change in the distribution of private resources.

Changes in Spatial Organization

The city is organized spatially to facilitate public provision. In general, schools, freeways, school catchment areas, boundaries, fire stations, one-way streets, and job opportunities are provided to a localized population. Accessibility to the population to be served, therefore, becomes an important criterion in locational policy. It is clear, however, that the facilitation permitted by spatial organization need not be equally satisfactory to all groups. In fact, as we have seen earlier in the book, those electors investing more in lobbying and other forms of information provision tend to prevail and to design that spatial organization in a way which provides them with a disproportionate share of the public cake.

Two elements of that spatial organization are readily apparent and will be treated here from the policy viewpoint. First, the spatial organization of urban political systems can be described in terms of a set of territories. These territories are de facto, as in the case of the lower-class slum, or de jure, as in the case of the independent suburb, and belong to a hierarchy, to the different levels of which public functions are assigned either explicitly or implicitly. As we remarked earlier, the relationship of territorial boundaries to the underlying population and the characteristics of that population (in terms of income, color, etc.) assume considerable importance for the equity of public provision. The assignment of public provision to different levels of the territorial hierarchy has a similar significance.

Second, we need to consider a set of point and line locations which function as sources of positive or negative externalities for their neighborhoods: shopping facilities, schools, highways, fire stations, employment facilities, incinerators, individual households, etc. These clearly need to be located in the context of the territorial organization of the city. Schools located on the boundary between a white and a black area perform altogether differently from the equity standpoint than do schools located in the centers of white and black areas respectively.

In brief, the problem is to design a spatial organization which will facilitate public allocation in an equitable and efficient manner. This requires the joint location of a hierarchy of territories and of certain discrete facilities to serve those territories. Here, we treat that organization and the location of public facilities separately. We then turn and examine the need to coordinate these locational policies in an overall strategy designed to mitigate current urban problems.

De Jure Territorial Organization

Consider first the question of de jure territorial organization where the territories have been assigned the legal right to provide themselves with certain public goods. Two apparently contradictory policies have been proposed in this regard: (1) *metropolitan integration* and (2) *community control*. On the one hand, therefore, we have policies aiming at the eradication of those municipal boundaries which currently fragment metropolitan areas. On the other hand, there are proposals for increasing that fragmentation particularly in the central city where such fragmentation, hitherto, has been relatively reduced in magnitude.

Each of these two types of policy is discussed in turn from three viewpoints: (1) the advantages from the equity and efficiency standpoints of achieving the goals emphasized by the policy; (2) the disadvantages with the same criteria in mind; and (3) the feasibility of such a policy; that is, could it be acceptable to a winning coalition within the contemporary American city?

Metropolitan Integration. Proponents of metropolitan integration advocate the replacement of governmental fragmentation within metropolitan areas by one metro-government which would be responsible for all the functions—education, police, highway maintenance, fire services, etc.—currently assigned to those individual municipalities. The new government would be elected on a one-man, one-vote principle—clearly there is scope for negotiation here. Integration, for example, might be made more acceptable to affluent suburbs by a territorial representation system in which the independent suburbs retained an identity as constituencies of the new metropolitan area and might even have a majority of city councilors.

The advantages of metropolitan integration are very apparent and are of such a magnitude that the sources of opposition are also quite predictable. First, and most importantly, integration would result in the elimination of the central-city–suburban fiscal disparities problem. The currently under-utilized tax resources of wealthy suburbs would be applied to the satisfaction of currently unmatched needs for public goods and services—

particularly education—within the central city. This obviously would involve an increased property tax rate in most suburbs in order to facilitate such a transfer of funds.

Second and more specifically, and to the extent that a problem exists, integration would largely eliminate suburban exploitation of the central city by bringing into congruence: (a) the territory consuming and (b) the territory funding the provision of a particular public good.

Additional advantages are also apparent and concern the locational pattern of externality-producing discrete facilities and households within the metropolitan area. Many of the negative externalities which independent suburbs currently impose on central cities result from their ability to compete, and to compete successfully, for employment opportunities and middle-class households. The first is achieved by means of offering tax concessions to industries and the second largely by discriminatory zoning. This, of course, can considerably aggravate the fiscal disparity problem by isolating central-city populations both from sources of employment and from high assessed property values. The replacement of such competition by a metropolitan monopoly of locational assignment via discriminatory tax and zoning policies could permit a much more equitable allocation. The transfer of zoning power from independent municipality to metro-government is especially important in this regard though metro-government, as a result of its abrogation of taxing power, would considerably reduce the incentives for a decentralization of zoning power.

Third, and finally, metropolitan integration would increase technical efficiency in the provision of some specific public goods. It is apparent that considerable economies of scale exist in the provision of some public goods so that provision for a larger population (up to a certain level) requires a smaller tax payment per consumer than does provision for a smaller population. This is very clear in the provision of public goods such as mosquito control, water, or sewage. As an example, it costs $58 per million gallons to provide primary sewage treatment in a facility with a million gallon capacity; it costs less than half this, however, in a facility with a capacity of 10 million gallons.[3] Such savings could permit the reallocation of tax resources to the satisfaction of demands for those services which the independent suburbs are most concerned about maintaining at their current levels of output: education is the primary case in point.

The efficiency of metropolitan integration, however, would depend very much on the way in which it is implemented. The argument presented above assumes that in an integrated metropolitan area a winning coalition would be prepared to, for example, rezone to the advantage of underprivileged central-city populations. Such would not necessarily be the case, particularly given what we can expect about the nature of that winning coalition. This is highly pertinent for a number of central cities in the U.S. where blacks have already achieved or are about to achieve a

---

[3] Bernard J. Frieden, *Metropolitan America: Challenge to Federalism*, Washington, D.C.: U.S. Government Printing Office, 1966, p. 30.

majority of the electorate. This places them clearly within reach of obtaining a majority coalition and, therefore, of a public reallocation within the central city from which ghetto areas can benefit. This prospect considerably reduces the attractiveness of a metro-government option.

This sectional interest brings us to a consideration of the acceptability of metro-government proposals to urban electorates. Judging from past successes in this area, one can hardly be optimistic. Very few proposals for the reorganization of urban government along metropolitan lines have passed the critical electoral test; even then the resultant metropolitan constitution has often been hedged with restrictions which vitiate the egalitarian aims of metropolitan integration. Indianapolis now includes not only the central city of Indianapolis but also the surrounding suburban municipalities within Marion County. However, the whole project makes a mockery of the concept of integration, by excluding the all-important functional area of education.

This affords an obvious clue, historically at least, to the geographical distribution of support and opposition for metropolitan integration within metropolitan areas. Generally, the more affluent middle-class suburbs with their lower tax rates and more ample public provision, particularly in education, have stood to lose from integration while poorer central-city populations with higher tax rates and inferior provision have stood to gain. In other words, metropolitan integration involved the imposition of negative political externalities on the populations of independent suburbs, something which obviously they have not cared to countenance. Today, for reasons such as their growing majority status, central-city black populations are increasingly disenamoured of the prospect of metropolitan integration. Opposition now assumes a more symmetrical character with respect to central city and independent suburb. As we shall see later, however, there do seem to be ways of designing territorial organizations which will permit metropolitan integration, but at the same time go a long way toward alleviating ghetto misgivings.

Community Control. Community control policies propose a greater fragmentation of legal authority within the metropolitan area than currently exists and have been advocated largely by ghetto representatives. Generally, community control proposals have called for at least two types of policy innovation. First, the devolution of authority to provide public services from the city to a smaller scale neighborhood level; such proposals have been largely concerned with decentralization of authority in the provision of education and police protection. Second, there have been demands for local community control and development of employment opportunities: this has been seen not only as a means of mitigating ghetto unemployment problems but also as a means of nurturing the development of a black entrepreneurial class. The latter calls for more extended treatment.

Community control and the development of employment opportunities within the ghetto have been pursued concurrently, with many businesses being established, owned, and operated by the people of the neighborhood for the benefit of the local community as a whole. In New York City, the Bedford-Stuyvesant Community Corporation Center owns a drugstore and a gas station; the profits from these are used to provide a social service, namely, a day care center. Similar in character is NEGRO, a black community-financed group which owns a hospital, a textile mill, a paint factory, a construction company, several apartment buildings, and two bus lines.[4]

The idea of community control and development of employment opportunities has received a measure of legislative legitimacy and stimulus from the proposed Community Development Corporation Act. This has found its way into the programmatic statements of the Republican and Democratic parties alike. The bill would establish community-controlled Community Development Corporations which, first, would own a group of businesses along the lines of NEGRO described above; and second, would invest between 20 percent and 80 percent of their profits in the provision of public services for the immediate neighborhood. The first function of the proposed Corporations would be expedited by attracting private capital into the community which, in return for tax incentives, would establish businesses there, train black labor and management, and ultimately transfer ownership to the Corporation.

Such community-sponsored development would obviously go a long way toward increasing the taxable resources available within poorer sections of a metropolitan area and particularly within the ghetto. Major interest, however, has been in the first form of community control discussed above: local control of the right to provide such services as education for areas no larger than, say, those occupied by the black ghetto. The advantages of such community control from the equity viewpoint are considerable.

First, it would provide ghetto control of the provision of public goods which ghetto inhabitants feel have been allocated in a spatially biased manner and to their detriment. This belief seems to be valid with respect to both education and police, as we have seen in the last chapter. Also, to the extent that decentralization of responsibility resulted in greater equity in the provision of education, it would help effect an equality of those private resources which are so important in the allocation process in the metropolitan area at large. The decentralization of the political process to the local level would have the same effect in that it would provide political experience to groups which have hitherto lacked it.

Second, decentralization of authority in areas such as education and police protection has been linked by some advocates with the demand for community development of employment opportunities. It would, for instance, be accompanied by decentralization of authority for contracting with private business. This could provide not only a stimulus to black-owned businesses in, say, the construction trade, but also some economic

---

[4] Elizabeth Howe, "Community Control," in Leonard J. Duhl (ed.), *A Symposium on the Urban Crisis,* Berkeley: Center for Planning and Development Research, University of California, 1968, p. 332.

leverage to be applied against discriminatory labor practices. With reference to the first point, it is noteworthy that in New York City between 1945 and 1968 over 95 percent of major construction in ghetto areas of the city was publicly funded or subsidized; yet not one prime contract was let to a minority-owned construction firm. In like manner, discriminatory labor practices have been publicly aided and abetted. It has been a frequent practice for public vocational high schools, therefore, to operate apprenticeship programs jointly with labor unions and to permit the unions to exclude black students from them. Black control of contracting to private business would provide some means at least of exercising a countervailing pressure against blatant inequity of this sort.

A major disadvantage of community control frequently voiced by its opponents is that of the implied loss of economies of scale. Large school and police systems, it is argued, can obtain economies in, for example, the procurement of supplies which are not available to small systems. In answer to this objection, however, two points can be raised. First, and most importantly in the particular cases of education and police, community control may produce an increase rather than a decrease in efficiency. It can hardly be said, for instance, that present tensions between civil servants and the public, particularly within the ghetto, are conducive to the effective delivery of public goods.[5] And second, a point that must be confronted if those demanding community control are to believe in equitable treatment, community control has always existed in independent suburban municipalities. For most central-city whites, moreover, such community control could be obtained simply by relocating, while for blacks this has only rarely been feasible. If community control is inefficient, why has it been permitted in the suburbs?

A second major disadvantage of community control is the problem of funding. If in the case of education, for example, control of funding as well as of expenditure, hiring, and curricular matters were delegated to the local level, the poorer communities which are the most enthusiastic in the demand for community control would command a rather meager platter. It is possible that a number of advocates would prefer this to no community control at all. The alternatives do not have to be structured in this way, however. There seems to be no fundamental reason, for instance, why funding and expenditure decisions should be made at the same territorial level. Certainly, much of the tax funds raised by the federal government are spent by territories at lower levels in the territorial hierarchy and with considerable local discretion as to the manner of that spending.

Nevertheless, wherever it has been raised the issue of community control has tended to be a hot one. In New York City, for example, early efforts at decentralization in the form of the ill-fated Ocean Hill-Brownsville demonstration project ran afoul of a city-wide teachers' union; there ensued a clear polarization of population preferences along racial lines. In

[5] Alan A. Altshuler, *Community Control,* New York: Pegasus, 1970.

a Louis Harris poll carried out in 1968, one month after the teachers' strike, a sample of school parents were asked whom they had supported, the community representatives or the union. Blacks supported the community by a ratio of 8 to 1 while whites supported the union by a ratio of 6 to 1.[6] In a broader question on the issue of community control—"Generally, do you feel that the community has too much influence in the running of the schools in this neighborhood, too little influence or just about the right amount of influence. . .?"—80 percent of black respondents who had an opinion felt the community had too little influence; comparable proportions for Jews and white Roman Catholics were 51 percent and 30 percent respectively.[7] Black support for community control also is reflected in the public pronouncements of black and civil rights groups such as the NAACP and the National Urban League.

While white groups would almost certainly be opposed, it seems that in the area of education at least a useful log-rolling operation could be carried out. This might involve, for example, a white acceptance of community control in exchange for a black rejection of busing. Certainly, decentralization of control of education would increase the bureaucratic problems of busing; such a tradeoff seems to have emerged in the case of community control in Detroit.[8]

In addition to the possibility of white opposition to community control, however, there are other important lobbies which need to be taken into account. These include the big city public bureaucracies, the public service labor unions, and the vendors who have held contracts from city education and safety departments in the past. In the case of community control of education, most of the opposition seems to be located in the teachers' unions: this is largely a result of concern over job security and also over promotion since the latter is facilitated by long-term employment at the same school. Community control would probably vitiate both of these goals by leading, in ghetto schools at least, to the replacement of white teachers by black teachers.

With respect to vendors, it is almost certain that some would be hurt by community control while neighborhood businesses would benefit. As a result, it is highly possible that vendors would form an important lobby opposed to community control. The blow could be cushioned, however, by gradual rather than immediate decentralization of purchasing power.

Community Control and Metropolitan Integration. Setting aside the problem of public acceptability, consider now the compatibility of the two policies. Seemingly they are incompatible in that metropolitan integration aims to eliminate fragmentation of metropolitan government while community control aims to increase it. This, however, would be an

---

[6] Ibid., p. 60.

[7] Ibid, pp. 59-60.

[8] William R. Grant, "Community Control vs. School Integration in Detroit," *Public Interest,* no. 24, Summer, 1971, pp. 62-79.

extremely facile view. Both policies have important contributions to make from the equity standpoint, and they are contributions that can be complementary rather than contradictory. Metropolitan integration, therefore, can make a contribution to equity by equalizing the funds available for public purposes throughout the metropolitan area. Community control, on the other hand, could assist by eliminating spatial bias in the spending of those funds.

Compatability between the two broad policies emerges from a recognition of two facts: first, that de jure territories belong to hierarchies with different functions being assigned to different levels of the hierarchy; and second, that the level at which a function can best be carried out from the equity standpoint varies from one function to another. It is obviously the case, in the current context, that equity in funding is best secured by a large territory at the level of the metropolitan area as a whole; equity in spending, however, is probably best served by devolution to smaller, local-level territories.

The Distribution of Households and Public Facilities

The second facet of the spatial organization of the metropolitan political system consists of those localized activities having externality effects and, therefore, an ability to provide public benefits or to impose public costs. Industrial activities, for instance, provide the positive externality of employment opportunity. Middle-class households provide the externality effects of high assessed valuations; the middle-class household also provides the externalities of reduced crime and desirable behavior patterns for those in its vicinity. Still other externality effects are manifested in the schools: contact with the highly motivated, the healthy and the socially esteemed.

Given the uneven geographical distribution of these externality-producing activities throughout a metropolitan area, clear problems of equity are posed. Not everyone lives in a middle-class residential area nor close to his place of work. Likewise, not every child can attend a school which has a largely middle-class enrollemnt and not all citizens can obtain access to the high assessed property values of the middle class.

Expressed another way, the equity problem is one of accessibility. Those who live close to middle-class people are likely to be better off in a variety of respects than those who live adjacent to a slum. Their physical security is likely to be enhanced, for instance, and their children will benefit from the additional school expenditures which middle-class PTAs seem to be able to obtain for their children. In like manner, the household residing in a middle-class suburban municipality will almost certainly benefit from more adequate provision of public services for a lower cost in property tax terms than will the central-city household.

Changes in territorial organization discussed above provide one broad policy approach toward altering those accessibility relationships which are so critical from the equity viewpoint. Metropolitan integration, for example, would go a long way toward equalizing accessibility to the externalities of high assessed property values. In this treatment, however, the major focus is on changing the accessibility relationships of externality-producing and localized activities independent of the territorial context.

Given this broad rubric, two general policy approaches to the accessibility problem remain. First, accessibility relationships can be changed by short-term movements between different parts of the metropolitan area on a larger scale than currently exists. As a stimulus to such movement, designed to effect greater equality in access to positive externalities, recourse is made to public transportation policies.

Second, instead of taking the distribution of externality-producing and localized activities as given and altering accessibility relationships by manipulating movement, accessibilities and inequities can be altered and alleviated respectively by changing the distribution itself. This is clearly the rationale which underlies the policy of opening up the suburbs to low-income, central-city populations and which also sustains proponents of urban renewal policies.

Specifically, therefore, three policy alternatives need to be considered: public transportation, opening up the suburbs and urban renewal. Each is considered in turn from the viewpoint of what is involved, its positive impact on the urban crisis, its limitations, and its public acceptability.

Public Transportation Policies. Public transportation policies have included both improvements in mass transit designed to alleviate the employment accessibility problem for central-city dwellers, and school busing designed to alleviate problems of racial imbalance within schools. Both policies approach the urban crisis by allowing people to reside where they are presently and transporting daily the disadvantaged to those areas which provide positive externalities not available at their original locations. In the case of school busing, of course, there has also been transportation of the advantaged to schools in disadvantaged neighborhoods with the same purpose in mind.

School Busing: The immediate objective of school busing policies is to satisfy some criterion of racial balance in pupil composition throughout the different schools making up a school system. The more long-term goal, on the other hand, is to provide an equality of education for the pupils within the same system. The idea that equality is not present in school systems where racial composition is highly variable derives from at least two ideas. First, there is the fact that, as we have seen earlier in this book, black schools tend to receive lower allocations of money, less experienced teachers, etc., than white schools. And second, there is the notion that contact with advantaged children is an important aspect of equality of education opportunity. Implicit in the Coleman report, for example, is the belief that children from disadvantaged backgrounds will show marked achievement gains when attending schools where a large proportion of the pupils are from more advantaged backgrounds.

The original legal impetus for busing came from the 1954 Supreme Court decision that racially segregated schools cannot be considered equal under the standards of the Fourteenth Amendment. Where segregation is clearly de jure, as it was in most of the South, court orders for integration were rapidly imposed and busing of pupils between schools in black and white areas of cities was the strategy adopted to achieve integration. Integration has usually been embodied in the form of some quantitative criterion of what constitutes racial balance in the schools of a school system. Usually this has been the proportion of total pupil composition which is black so that busing aims to achieve an equality in this proportion in all schools in a system.

Outside of the South, the presence of de jure segregation has been much more difficult to establish; court orders to integrate have turned upon the difficult distinction between de jure and de facto segregation in schools. The distinction, as presently defined in the Fourteenth Amendment, revolves around the issue of discrimination wherever expressed officially and administratively through official administrative policy. In many cities, there is segregation which without investigation could have been dismissed as de facto but which on investigation has proved to be the result of official discriminatory action; this then has to be undone by court order.

Theoretically, the busing solution has much to recommend it. It should, for example, reduce incentives to the unequal allocation of resources in schools within the same school system. In addition, it should promote beneficial contacts between lower-income blacks and higher-income whites with both gaining from the exchange in terms of motivation and interracial understanding. Apparently, however, theory has been deceptive since the introduction of busing tends to set in motion certain other changes resulting in resegregation and the gradual fiscal deprivation of the integrated school system.

Generally, the white, more affluent sections of the urban population have been opposed to busing and integration. This has prompted one of two strategies: (1) remove the child to a private school; in the South private schools have been dubbed segregation academies though clearly not all of them are racially segregationist in intent and (2) relocate to the suburbs where the school systems tend to be lily-white. Both strategies have the long-term effect of vitiating the objective of court-ordered integration. In addition, withdrawal to private schools reduces the incentive for the white parent to vote positively on requests for increased public education expenditures. Further, relocation to the suburbs aggravates the central-city–suburban fiscal disparities problem.

Also, over the short term, busing rarely seems successful in achieving its objectives. Within schools, streaming may be adopted with the blacks being assigned—often justifiably in terms of achievement tests—to the slowest streams. The reception accorded minority blacks in white majority schools has often been less than cordial and reports of interracial conflict have been widespread. In addition, a recent report from cities in the North and South showed that large numbers of black students in newly integrated schools had been suspended.[9] To the vast majority of whites, therefore, busing is clearly not acceptable and has resulted in parents voting with their feet or alternatively devising ways of vitiating integration goals within the schools themselves.

The mood has been contagious. Blacks are no longer optimistic about attaining educational equity via the busing strategy and have increasingly resorted to isolationist policies such as the community control movement. It should occasion little surprise, therefore, that ghettoes are willing to trade a segregated educational system for community control. This has been the solution adopted in Detroit and there is evidence of this coalition of white and black interests elsewhere in the country; a plan for community control in Los Angeles, for instance, was jointly sponsored in the California legislature by a conservative white senator and a black senator from the Watts area.[10]

Mass Transit Improvements: Conceptually akin to busing policies in the area of access to quality education is the policy of improving mass transit services in order to improve the access of low-income, central-city dwellers to suburban job opportunities. Subsidy of mass transit systems in such a context assumes that there is a "transportation-and-poverty" problem in which central-city unemployment is a function of the inaccessibility of suburban employment opportunities. Theoretically, therefore, improvement of such accessibility should widen the area over which the unemployed can search for and ultimately hold down a job.

In theory, the idea is attractive. It is also acceptable electorally in that it does not involve the residential and educational contact with blacks from which whites shrink. In addition, it is frequently supported by the downtown business elite as a means of maintaining central-city attractiveness.

Projected mass transit systems seem unlikely to alter this accessibility problem. The much publicized Bay Area Rapid Transit System in the San Francisco Bay area, for example, will have 75 route miles and 37 stations; yet only 8 of those miles and 11 of the stations will be in San Francisco itself.[11] This is true despite the fact that 75 percent of the occupied housing units in the San Francisco-Oakland SMSA lacking an automobile are within San Francisco. Further, the trains are planned so as to pass through the ghettos only incidentally. Hunter's Point is not on the

---

[9] *The New York Times,* September 5, 1971.

[10] *Hearings Before the Select Committee on Equal Educational Opportunitity of the United States Senate, 91st Congress, 2nd Session on Equal Educational Opportunity, Part 6—Racial Imbalance in Urban Schools,* 1970, p. 3109.

[11] Martin Wohl, "Public Transportation and Income Groups," in David M. Gordon (ed.), *Problems in Political Economy: An Urban Perspective,* Lexington, Mass.: D.C. Heath, 1971, pp. 435-436.

route network and there are no stations in the Oakland ghettos. Similar patterns of concentration in residential areas housing other than the urban poor seem characteristic of the rapid transit systems planned for Los Angeles and Atlanta.[12]

While theoretically, metropolitan mass transit systems should be in the interests of both central-city poor requiring access to suburban jobs and the downtown business elite desirous of business expansion, there has been something of a conflict of interest in terms of specific network design. The downtown business elite appears to have won, thus vitiating the utility of mass transit for low-income, central-city populations.[13]

Opening Up the Suburbs. The basic idea here is to mitigate the gross inequities associated with the current spatial allocation of public goods and accessibility to localized externality-producing activities by facilitating a massive relocation of lower-income groups and blacks from the disadvantaged central-city locations of metropolitan areas to the more advantaged suburban locations. This facilitation is to be accomplished specifically by a threefold attack: first, the elimination of discriminatory housing markets which hinder blacks from movement out of the ghettoes; second, elimination of discriminatory zoning by independent suburbs, which serves to keep lower-income groups out regardless of race; and third, a vast expansion of public housing so that housing can be made available at reasonable cost in suburban areas. Changes of this magnitude, however, are likely to come about only through new legislation and a massive effort to enforce both the provisions of that new legislation and those of the constitution; the provisions of the Fourteenth Amendment regarding equal protection under the law are particularly applicable in this regard.

The general advantages of opening up the suburbs are very evident. First, it will reduce the disparities in financial needs and resources between central city and suburb and so go a long way toward eliminating the central-city–suburban fiscal disparities problem from which current big city financial crises largely derive. Second, apart from a balancing of the ledger, however, there would also be greater equity in such intangibles as access to crime-free environments, to employment opportunities, and, for the children, to the better-motivated children of the largely middle-class suburban schools. Third, opening up the suburbs to low-income groups would serve to make the suburbs less attractive to the middle class, slow down white middle-class flight to the suburbs and hence move the constituent territories of the metropolitan system to some sort of balance between fiscal needs and resources.

The purist may demur that the disadvantage of this happy state of affairs would be a reduced demand for a rationalization of territorial organization and a consequent loss of the benefits of increased efficiency

[12] Wohl, op. cit., p. 436.

[13] See, for example, Danny Beagle, Al Haber and David Wellman, "Rapid Transit – The Case of BART," in Gordon, op. cit., pp. 437-439.

likely to stem from metropolitan government. This may be so, but it seems unlikely. Opening up the suburbs would result in a gradual convergence in levels of public provision between central city and independent suburb and, therefore, eliminate the source of current suburban opposition to territorial integration.

The legal and constitutional mandates and the legal precedents for a policy of opening up the suburbs clearly exist. That the will to enforce them has not always been present to the same degree is evidence of sensitivity to a public opinion largely opposed to such policies and particularly when it involves immediate neighborhoods.

Most important in the armory of legislation, which an aggressive administration can draw on, is Title VIII of the 1968 Federal Civil Rights Act, elsewhere termed the Fair Housing Act. The most critical provisions of that act from our viewpoint are: (1) that discrimination in the sale and rental of housing, in the financing of housing, and in the provision of brokerage services is illegal; and (2) that all executive departments and agencies of the federal government are to administer their programs relating to housing and urban development in a manner affirmatively to further equal housing opportunities.

In addition to this legislation, however, it is also possible to file legal suits in cases involving discriminatory zoning by appealing to the equal protection clause of the Fourteenth Amendment. An interesting case in this respect involved a nonprofit housing sponsor and the city of Lawton, Oklahoma, in 1970. The immediate dispute arose from sponsor efforts to secure zoning for multifamily residences so as to enable construction of a federally subsidized housing project in a white section of Lawton. The Lawton city council refused to rezone, whereupon a suit was filed with the Tenth Circuit Court. The court found that the particular zoning decision was the direct result of racial discrimination and that it violated equal protection rights as specified by the Fourteenth Amendment.[14]

The equal protection argument has been shown to have equal validity in overcoming exclusionary building permit policies in addition to negating exclusionary zoning policies. In August, 1970, the Federal District Court in New York ruled that Lackawanna, New York, had violated equal protection rights by using a claimed sewer emergency to thwart a low-income housing development planned for a white neighborhood of that city.[15] Such cases are by no means isolated; there is, in fact, an accumulating body of precedents which provide the basis for a full-scale attack on exclusionary zoning, building code, and building permit policies.

Despite this impressive battery of constitutional and legal provision and precedent, however, administrative policy in enforcing the law has been faltering at best. Given the predominantly Republican complexion of the

[14] *Hearings Before the Select Committee on Equal Educational Opportunity of the United States Senate, 91st Congress, 2nd Session on Equal Educational Opportunity, Part 5—De Facto Segregation and Housing Discrimination,* 1970, p. 2921.
1970, p. 2921.
[15] Ibid., p. 2922.

suburban areas, this sensitivity on the part of the currently Republican administration is perhaps not surprising.

On the one hand, there have been administrative acts suggesting determination to open up the suburbs to the deprived. This is evident in administration plans for expanding the supply of public housing along with the specification of criteria for site selection. When the Nixon administration took office in 1969, production of subsidized housing was at a meager 200,000 units a year. Yearly production has now been increased above the half million mark. Such programs are administered by HUD and while that department does not build housing or select sites—these are at the discretion of local public and private organizations—it can reject sites chosen. Perhaps the most significant criterion pursued is that additions to public housing in areas of minority racial concentration should be avoided. This is at least consistent with the policy of opening up the suburbs.

Also significant have been isolated indications of HUD's willingness to use its financial and legal power to secure the equal opportunity provisions of the 1968 Civil Rights Act. In the case of Warren, a suburban municipality in the Detroit area, for example, funds for a low-income housing project were withheld because local authorities refused to guarantee nondiscrimination in the allocation of the units. Also, in the Blackjack case referred to in Chapter Three, HUD has taken action against exclusionary zoning by asking the Justice Department to file suit against the municipality employing the tactic.

Nevertheless, despite these specific cases, the general use by HUD of the powers available to it have not been reassuring to those who wish to see a dispersal of the disadvantaged into the suburban areas of American cities. For example, there has been a reluctance to join with and assist those filing suits against discriminatory zoning. A case in point concerned Union City in California: SASSO, the Southern Alameda Spanish-Speaking Organization, attempted to secure a rezoning of land to build multifamily housing. They were legally represented by the National Committee Against Discrimination in Housing which unsuccessfully asked the Department of Justice and HUD to join them in the case. Interestingly enough, the outcome of the case represented a success for the plaintiffs: the District court, while refusing rezoning, ordered Union City to come up with a plan to resolve all its housing needs within ten months.[16]

Elsewhere, the public pronouncements of representatives of HUD reveal an unwillingness to withhold funds in an effort to exert leverage in discriminatory zoning cases; Secretary George Romney, for instance, and despite his action in the case of Warren, Michigan, has expressed the opinion that to do so might interfere with the constitutional right of states to zone land and to delegate the right to zone land as they see fit.[17] Similar sensitivity to a public opinion generally adverse to the policy of opening up the suburbs is apparent in two other areas: (1) enforcement of

[16] Ibid., p. 2914.
[17] Ibid., pp. 2790-2791.

current antihousing discrimination legislation and (2) the locational policies of federal agencies themselves

With respect to the first point and to the housing provisions of the
1968 Civil Rights Act, it is significant that HUD has no cease-and-desist
powers in considering individual complaints of violation. This has served
to discourage victims of discrimination from applying to HUD for redress,
thus weakening the effectiveness of the law. Indeed, HUD's role is limited
to that of persuasion and it cannot take legal action itself even though, as
a result of a complaint, it may investigate and gather an appreciable
amount of information about the case at issue. Yet, a large body of
experience in enforcing legislative provisions has indicated that the most
effective way to enforce a law against discrimination is to establish an
independent agency to hold hearings on complaints of violation and to
issue cease-and-desist orders.

The Department of Justice, on the other hand, is empowered to bring
suits in cases of discrimination and has indeed brought a number, most of
them ending in consent decrees. The consent decrees obtained, however,
constitute a mere drop in the bucket relative to the overall magnitude of
housing discrimination. In addition, and as a result of lack of resources,
the Department of Justice has not handled all the cases brought to it by
individual complainants. In a case reported in the *Los Angeles Times,* the
Department of Justice responded only after a two-year delay to a
complaint brought by the Washington office of the American Civil
Liberties Union regarding housing discrimination in a large Maryland
recreational project. The response was that while the case had been
investigated and that indeed there were indications of discrimination the
Department lacked the manpower to justify trying to enforce compliance
with the 1968 Civil Rights Act.[18]

The effect of such administrative reluctance to enforce federal law is to
shift the financial burden from society as a whole to the individual
complainant. The result has been a pitifully small number of successful
suits despite the generally recognized pervasiveness of housing discrimination. Not only is the initiation of legal suits costly but there is also a
notable reluctance on the part of local attorneys to enter into cases which
are often controversial and time-consuming. The fact that attorneys derive
much of their business from the real estate industry is also of the highest
relevance in this regard. In summary, therefore, it is as if fair housing
legislation was designed almost purely for its cosmetic value rather than
for its effectiveness in remedying those spatial patterns of households
which generate repetitive inequity.

Finally, the locational policies of federal agencies themselves are not
particularly helpful in this regard; they again suggest an unwillingness to
act in a way which, while contrary to the wishes of the white majority,
would advance the cause of equity across locations within metropolitan
areas. Large federal contracts, for instance, are given to firms which do

[18] Ibid., pp. 3081-3082.

little or nothing to secure open housing for their black employees in the vicinity of the plant. Federal funds are still channeled into independent suburban municipalities which have demonstrated resistance to housing desegregation. In addition, federal offices themselves are relocated without effort to secure housing in the neighborhood for minority employees. Two agencies of the Department of Health, Education and Welfare relocated to Rockville, Maryland taking approximately 6,500 jobs with them.[19] There was no effort to make nondiscriminatory housing available; rather, the major effort focused upon securing transportation with Washington, D.C. so that black employees could commute!

Urban Renewal. In many ways, urban renewal policies largely pursued by central cities represent the duality of the policies listed above: instead of opening up the suburbs to lower-income groups by breaking down current barriers to relocation, urban renewal aims to open up the central city to the suburban middle class by vastly increasing the residential attractiveness of sections of the central city.

The ideal has been that the replacement of blighted areas by modern apartment developments appealing to the middle class with a yen for the cultural attractions of the city would produce positive externalities for the city as a whole as a result of an increased property tax yield. In addition, though unstated, the problem-populations might just take their troubles elsewhere. The idea is theoretically attractive but has become progressively difficult to implement. First, the history of urban renewal legislation and guidelines has been one of increasing attentiveness to the needs of the displaced. This has been reflected in an increasing stress on: (a) rehabilitation rather than clearance; (b) adequate relocation assistance where clearance has taken place; and (c) neighborhood participation in the renewal process. These have reduced the attractiveness of urban renewal for hard-pressed city governments. In addition, the displaced populations have just not disappeared. Rather, they have been crowded into remaining slum areas, thus creating conditions of overcrowding and health hazard for the remainder of the city. Not only that, but they have shown themselves increasingly resistant to displacement in the first place.

While originally publicly acceptable, therefore, in the sense that the benefits tended to flow disproportionately to the downtown business elite and the white, middle class resuming residency in the new residential developments going up on the cleared sites, there have been increasing difficulties of implementation. As a result, the net effect of urban renewal upon the spatial arrangement of localized activities having externality effects has been rather limited.

Territorial Organization, Households and Public Facilities

A brief review of the material presented above, however, and an articulation of the ideas expressed regarding territorial organization and land use,

---

[19] Ibid., p. 2950.

respectively, should be sufficient to convince one that changes in territorial organization and changes in the pattern of localized, externality-
producing activities should be combined for maximum policy effectiveness. Two instances are particularly striking in this context.

First, it is apparent that the feasibility of busing to achieve racial
balance and to obtain some positive interaction between children of
different races is vitiated by the characteristic territorial fragmentation of
metropolitan areas. The likely benefits of busing which we reiterated
above are unlikely to be accomplished in a territorial context where
escape from a heavily black central city into a lily-white independent
suburb is so easy. Nor are busing agreements between suburban and
central-city school systems likely. Indeed, one of the reasons for the
independent middle-class suburb is precisely this insulation effect.

A second case concerns the residential opening up of suburbs to
lower-income groups. This policy would clearly be facilitated by rezoning
of residential land in independent suburbs from single-family, large-lot
residences to multifamily residences. Rezoning, in turn, would be greatly
facilitated by a more centralized control of zoning policy—the type of
centralized control associated with metropolitan integration and the
vesting of the zoning rights of suburbs in a new metropolitan government.

Clearly, these types of change are extremely difficult to institute simply
because: (a) they are maximally effective in mitigating the urban crisis;
(b) certain individuals have a vested interest in the conditions which have
produced the urban crisis; and (c) the suggested policies are so obviously
related to the elimination of those conditions. The third reason, however,
prompts consideration of more subtle approaches which, while not
explicitly directed at the urban crisis, would be of great utility in
mitigating it. Three examples of such policies are considered here.

First, a national policy with respect to urban size would be of
appreciable value. The problems of inequity which have been described in
this volume are disproportionately problems of larger metropolitan areas
rather than of smaller metropolitan areas. Major reasons for spatial
inequity include accessibility problems and the relationship between
segregation and the localized provision of public goods. Consider the
accessibility problem: in a larger city, the distance from the black ghetto
close to the downtown area to expanding employment opportunities in
the suburbs may be ten miles or more. In a small town, on the other hand,
the average distance separating ghetto resident from employment is likely
to be much smaller. Not only has suburbanization of employment
proceeded more slowly in small towns; where it has occurred, it still leaves
the employment opportunities highly accessible to central-city dwellers
simply because of the small areal extent of the city.

With reference to segregation of social and racial groups, it is apparent
that, even though the smaller city may be as segregated as the larger city,
the perverse effects of such segregation upon social contact are likely to
be reduced. For example, cities of, say, 50,000 inhabitants often have
only one high school; in cities of 500,000, on the other hand, there may

be several high schools, each one catering to a socially and/or racially segregated clientele. The implications for the need for such policies as racial busing should be obvious.

Quite how a national urban-size policy would be structured is not immediately evident. It might, however, assume the form of a New Town policy designed to reduce the migration pressures upon the larger metropolitan areas. A large number of towns in the 5,000-10,000 population range, for instance, might be chosen as the nuclei for such towns, with large amounts of federal money being channeled into them for the expansion of housing, public services, transportation, etc. A well-designed federal policy would be almost irresistible to so many towns in that population-size bracket, since they tend to have relatively slow rates of growth in population and wealth.

It will undoubtedly be argued that a policy of decentralization of urban growth runs counter to national economic growth policies. Many urban economists would argue, for instance, that the large metropolitan area provides a wide variety of positive externalities to business firms which are of critical significance for the growth of those firms.[20] This may be. It is also apparent, however, that while urban size may provide positive externalities of an economic nature, it has been responsible in part for the imposition of negative externalities of a social character. A reconsideration of priorities seems overdue.

A second broad policy change with subtle implications for amelioration of the urban problem is the elimination of the locally administered property tax as a means of funding locally provided public goods and services. Elimination of the locally administered property tax and replacement by, say, a state income tax would eliminate much of the impetus for exclusionary zoning so characteristic of middle-class independent suburbs. Exclusionary zoning is motivated largely by a desire to maximize the ratio of property tax base to population. Elimination of the property tax would eliminate the need for land-use policies which have such clearly perverse effects not only on those of modest income but also on the population at large: consider the effects of large-lot zoning on urban sprawl and the cost of federally subsidized highways, sewer lines, etc.

In addition, abrogation of the municipal right to tax by the state—an act which would be constitutionally legitimate—would permit a spatial redistribution of resources from municipalities which currently have large tax bases per capita to those which have relatively meager per capita tax bases. The implications of this for the mitigation of the urban fiscal disparities problem are readily apparent.

Nor is the elimination of the locally administered property tax as the basis for local funding mere "pie in the sky." In brief, it can be argued quite convincingly that the present financing arrangements of schools violate the "equal protection clause" of the Fourteenth Amendment. The argument runs as follows. The states are responsible for financing the

---

[20] William Alonso, "The Economics of Urban Size," *Papers and Proceedings of the Regional Science Association*, vol. 26, 1970.

schools. Hence, all taxes collected for education, whether collected by state or local districts, are considered to be state taxes, and if disparities exist in the revenue resources available to the local district they are judged to exist at the discretion of the state. If the state bases school financing on where the student lives or according to the wealth of his area, then the state is not giving equal protection of the law to all residents.

In line with this argument, a number of cities have already begun to sue their respective states to provide such equal protection. Some of these suits argue in terms of the state guaranteeing that each child in the public schools should receive a level of expenditures determined only by his educational needs. Still others ask to prevent the correlation of school district wealth with expenditures per pupil.

A third policy innovation with positive implications for urban problems would be a federally administered system of insurance for individual householders against loss of property values. A major fear of middle-class householders, concerning the social and/or racial integration of their neighborhoods, is that of property value deterioration. If this belief is sincere and not merely an ideological justification for racism or social snobbery, then a system of insuring householders against loss might be an effective weapon in the residential stabilization of neighborhoods.

What this implies, essentially, is a governmental subsidy to the middle class to live in the same neighborhoods as the lower class. A system of this type is operated by the British government by means of the admission criteria for public housing; these are extremely broad with respect to private income. Though the original notion was that Council housing (i.e., public housing) should benefit lower-income groups, this proviso was dropped from the law in 1949; since then the allocational criterion has been that of "housing need"—a criterion not necessarily related to low income. The outcome of this has been an allocation of Council housing which is relatively indifferent to income group up to the upper middle-class level. For example, the proportion of childless families with incomes of less than £6 per week living in Council housing in 1961 was the same as the proportion of those in the £14-20 income bracket. The effects of such allocation on residential integration *within* specific housing estates, however, has not been examined. Quite possibly, the aggregate figures mask social segregation *within* individual housing estates, thus vitiating the goal of providing middle-class positive externalities for lower-class residents.

All the policy measures discussed above have the quality of producing equitable locational change. Much broader policies of an explicitly nonlocational character, however, also have the property of instigating such desirable locational change. These policies concern redistribution of private resources and it is to these that we now turn.

Changes in the Redistribution of Private Resources

The major point which we wish to make in this second section is that changes in the redistribution of private resources have the capability of inducing greater equity in public provision and consequently in environmental quality across localized populations. A minor point is that such changes need not necessarily diminish the efficiency with which public goods are produced.

Spatial inequity in public provision is, as we have seen in this volume, strongly correlated with social inequity: the middle class tends to get more of the public benefits while those of lower income and the blacks get less. This outcome is contingent on a residential segregation of the middle class from the lower class and of the white from the black. Segregation by social class deprives the lower class and the black (both of whom tend to be largely lower income) from the external benefits which the middle class can bestow in schools and in neighborhoods; middle-class neighborhoods also seem more effective in competition for what the city has to offer. Other public benefits are of a more indirect character: the suburbanization of the middle class and of the white, for instance, has prompted the relocation of doctors and dentists out of the city and increased their inaccessibility to lower-income clienteles.

Given that segregation is a result of negative externalities seen by the middle class as imposed by the lower class, what is the source of those externalities and how might it be eliminated? Undoubtedly, as Smolensky and Gomery have outlined elsewhere, a major source of these negative externalities—particularly public behavior externalities—is the package of goods and services which the lower-income family is constrained to buy.[21] Less housing and space can be purchased, for instance, so that children must play in the streets to the annoynace of those less financially constrained. Less money can be set aside for maintenance of residential property, imposing negative externalities on neighbors who are able to afford such expenditures. And reduced financial resources are often associated with petty crime as a means of increasing resources—again imposing obvious externalities. It follows, therefore, that an important approach to eliminating the external costs which motivate segregation would be a redistribution of income so as to increase the private resources available to lower-income groups.

Social and racial segregation are not the only forces promoting inequity in environmental quality, however. Additional reasons lie in the power which the middle class and the white are able to mobilize with respect to the spatial organization of the urban political system—the location of obnoxious public land uses; the allocation of school resources across locations within the metropolitan area, etc. These forces also work in the direction of conferring greater public benefits on the higher-income groups and the white and reduced benefits on the lower income and the black. Again, one could argue that such power stems from the particular package of goods which higher income permits one to purchase: legal aid, for example, and leisure with which to attend public meetings and to obtain political experience as an officer. The policy imperatives, therefore,

---

[21] Eugene Smolensky and J. D. Gomery, "The Urban Problem as an Exercise in the Theory of Efficient Transfers," *Discussion Paper 100-71, Institute for Research on Poverty,* University of Wisconsin, Madison, Wisconsin, 1971.

would further point in the direction of a redistribution of private resources as a major means of alleviating the problem of spatial inequity in the city.

To some degree, efficiency criteria point in the same policy direction. Inequality in private resources is inefficient from the viewpoint of the production of public goods: fewer collective benefits are produced than conceivably would be the case with a more equitable distribution of private resources. A redistribution of private resources toward lower-income groups, for instance, could feasibly increase their productivity and their return to tax resources as a result of their purchase of improved housing, health and education.

In addition, greater redistribution of private resources might reduce the need for some public goods presently consuming public resources which could be used more beneficially for other purposes. Consider, for instance, the public costs of locationally adjusting to the negative externalities imposed by lower class on middle class—suburban sprawl, freeway construction, traffic congestion, the demise of mass transit systems. All impose costs on the public and consume resources which could be allocated to, say, education. Furthermore, many of these public expenditures, although benefitting disproportionately the middle class, are funded by a regressive tax system which imposes proportionately greater costs on lower-income groups. The Bay Area Rapid Transit System referred to above is a case in point.[22]

What precisely, are the policies which should be adopted in order to provide a more equitable distribution of private resources? Public taxation and expenditure policies can be characterized as to their regressiveness, and their regressiveness is an excellent indicator of the degree to which public policies redistribute income. Briefly, if the result of a public policy is to impose greater costs as a percentage of private income on lower-income groups and reduced proportional costs on higher-income groups, the policy may be regarded as regressive. Likewise, if benefits are perversely related to income such that groups of lower-income receive benefits which amount to a smaller proportion of their total income than is the case for higher-income groups, the policy may also be regarded as regressive. This is in contradistinction to the progressive situation where proportional benefits decrease with private income or where proportional costs increase. A major problem in monitoring income redistribution policies is that of evaluating regressiveness; with taxation policy this is less onerous than with expenditure policy. It is to the former, therefore, that we initially turn.

A virtually unanimous conclusion from studies which have examined the impact of state and local taxes is that they tend to be highly regressive in their incidence. Typically, for households with annual incomes of less than $5,000, state and local taxes as a percent of income are more than

---

[22] Martin Wohl, "Users of Urban Transportation Services and Their Income Circumstances," in *Conference on Transportation and Poverty: Report,* Brookline, Mass.: American Academy of Arts and Sciences, 1968.

twice as high as for those with incomes above $5,000. Indeed, for the very poorest households—those with annual incomes of less than $3,000—the percentage of income taken by state and local taxes is usually at least three times greater than for those with incomes above $5,000 per year.

The principal factor accounting for this regressivity is the locally administered property tax on housing. As shown in Table 2.2, such regressiveness is extremely steep at very low-income levels. This regressivity reflects the fact that housing expenditure is a very high proportion of current income for the poor. It should also be pointed out that this regressiveness has become even more pronounced since 1960.

Of much less significance in accounting for regressivity in the incidence of state and local taxes are the general sales taxes found in most states and cities. In addition to *general* sales taxes, all states and some municipalities impose *selective* sales taxes and excise taxes on such goods as liquor, tobacco, automobiles, and insurance premiums. Many of these taxes are not regressive since consumption of the taxed item increases with and more rapidly than family income. On the other hand, as Netzer has indicated, this lack of regressivity in many selective sales taxes emphasizes the failure of the poor to consume products which would help alleviate their poverty.[23] This is particularly true of such items as automobiles and automobile insurance.

Whatever progressiveness is apparent in taxation, therefore, is largely attributable to the progressive federal income tax. Our analysis suggests that if redistribution of private resources from middle class to lower class is to be taken further it will have to be by means of progressive income taxes. At what precise geographic scale they should be administered is a moot point and links up with much of what we have written regarding policies which are more explicitly locational in character.

There are important reasons of a tax-gathering machinery character, for example, which require that progressive income taxes be administered at a larger rather than at a smaller scale. In particular, the administration of a progressive income tax calls for a much more sophisticated tax collection and monitoring system than does the property tax. From the point of view of administration, the property tax is extremely cheap and does not require highly skilled tax collectors; this is one reason, of course, why it has been so popular at the local level.

In addition, however, tax collection on a large geographic scale would eliminate other sources of current urban conflict. It would prevent, for example, much of the tax rate competition which presently accounts for a great deal of the mobility of businesses—and to some extent of people—within metropolitan areas to the detriment of central-city populations. Further, and assuming that revenues were not distributed back to the local level in proportion to taxes gathered, it could result in an equalization of tax resources per capita across territories.

[23] Dick Netzer, "Tax Structures and Their Impact on the Poor," in John P. Crecine (ed.), *Financing the Metropolis,* Beverly Hills: Sage Publications, Inc., 1970, p. 471.

On the expenditure side, the incidence of benefits shows a distinct bias toward the poor and tends to lead to considerable redistribution from upper- to lower-income groups despite the regressiveness of state and local tax systems. Nevertheless, considerable regressiveness still remains, often so glaring as to make one contemplate how rapidly poverty might be eliminated as a result of greater progressiveness in the total tax-expenditure package.

An excellent case in point is provided by explicit and implicit housing subsidies. In 1962, housing subsidies to poor people in the form of rent subsidies for public housing, public assistance, and savings due to income tax deductions amounted to $820 million. The subsidy to middle-income groups, on the other hand, resulting from savings due to income tax deductions amounted to an astonishing $2.9 billion. Even more striking is a comparison of the $820 million subsidy provided to approximately the poorest 20 percent of the total population with the $1.7 billion provided to the wealthiest 20 percent.[24]

While housing provides a particularly well-documented case of redistributional perversity, it is probably not a solitary case. Almost certainly, for instance, one could document similar problems in the transportation area. Consider, for example, the effects of regressive taxes on automobiles, urban freeway systems subsidized by regressive tax systems, and inadequately subsidized public transport systems. There is no doubt, therefore, that appreciable scope exists for increased progressivity in public expenditures. Further, it is the contention here that such redistribution would have important homogenizing effects on the externalities which households provide for each other. Theoretically, such homogenization should be reflected in reduced segregation and in a more equitable allocation of public expenditures and land uses, be they beneficial or obnoxious.

Summary and Concluding Comments

The purpose of this chapter has been to discuss and to evaluate public policies directed at alleviating locational inequity in public provision and, consequently, in environmental quality within cities. The policies discussed have been not only the ones which currently preoccupy urban policy makers but also those which are at present conjectural but which might provide useful ameliorations of the grosser inequities of the urban environment.

Broadly, two types of policy have been discussed: those policies which proceed by *changing the spatial organization of the political system* directly; and those which aim to mitigate locational inequity by *changes in the allocation of private resources* among individuals within the urban political system.

An important component of spatial organization is the partition of the urban area into formal jurisdictions. Two policies have been proposed

[24] Alvin L. Schorr, "Housing the Poor," in Warner Bloomberg, Jr. and Henry J. Schmandt (eds.), *Urban Poverty: Its Social and Political Dimensions,* Beverly Hills: Sage Publications, Inc., 1968, pp. 231-232.

with respect to that de jure territorial organization. On the one hand, *metropolitan integration* would eliminate current jurisdictional fragmentation and would help in eliminating the central-city–suburban fiscal disparities problem by using the surplus tax capacity of the suburbs to satisfy presently unsatisfied public needs of central-city populations. It would consequently impose an increased burden on the populations of independent suburbs and has been opposed by them for that reason.

Alternatively, there have been demands for greater *community control* of certain functions such as education, police, and economic development. These policies involve increased jurisdictional fragmentation; they have been proposed largely by ghetto populations and opposed by white populations whose majority advantages in urban policy making would thereby be vitiated. It has been suggested that such community control would provide poor community school districts with a funding problem. As we pointed out, however, there is no necessary conflict between decentralized control of expenditure decisions and centralized control of revenue collection.

A second component of the spatial organization of the urban political system consists of the geographic pattern of those localized activities which have strong externality effects of either a positive or negative nature: middle-class households, schools, employment opportunities, etc. Generally, two approaches to that locational pattern are evident in current policy. First, there are those policies that leave that locational pattern as it is and improve the accessibility of the deprived on a daily journey-to-work or journey-to-school basis. Policies here have included those aimed at providing *improved mass transit facilities between the ghetto and suburban employment opportunities;* and also the much maligned *busing of pupils to achieve racial balance.*

Second are those policies which aim to change accessibility relationships for the deprived by changing the locational pattern itself. Major national emphasis here recently has been on the policy of "opening up the suburbs" to lower-income groups and blacks to provide greater accessibility to employment opportunities, and proximity to middle-class, white populations. The effectiveness of this policy depends on a vast increase in public housing and the elimination of discriminatory zoning and of discriminatory housing markets. The first condition appears to be on its way to fulfillment while the other two have proven more difficult to realize.

Alternatives to opening up the suburbs are represented by investment in *mass transit* and *urban renewal.* Policies of urban renewal have had as one of their aims an increase in middle-class residential land uses within the central city. Increasing opposition of the lower-class populations to be moved, however, has led to much greater emphasis recently on rehabilitation as opposed to renewal.

Clearly, policies designed to change accessibility to sources of externalities and those aimed at changing the territorial organization of the urban political system partly depend on one another for their effectiveness. As long as metropolitan integration is utopian, therefore, the effectiveness of busing to achieve racial balance within central cities will be vitiated by white flight.

It was also suggested that other policies aimed at eliminating the conditions which provide raison d'êtres for the public and private actions generating the contemporary urban problem might be more effective. These included a *national urban growth policy* aimed at channeling urban growth into smaller rather than larger urban centers; *elimination of the locally administered property tax;* and *a federally administered system of insurance for individual householders against loss of property values* resulting from third-party effects.

The second broad category of policies include those directed toward altering the allocation of private resources as a prerequisite to greater locational equity. The argument here is twofold; first, higher-income groups currently are much more likely to undertake effective action to preserve or enhance the residential attractiveness of their neighborhoods; second, incomes control those aspects of private consumption which have externality effects and, therefore, the residential acceptability of different income groups. Both factors tend to work to the detriment of lower-income groups.

Current taxation and public expenditure policies can be characterized with respect to their progressiveness or regressiveness. Important elements of regressiveness still exist and need to be eliminated. Locally administered property and sales taxes, therefore, should be reduced relative to the progressive federal income tax. On the benefit side, considerable progressiveness exists. Nevertheless, there are some glaring discrepancies; the housing subsidy to private home buyers implicit in federal income tax deductions is an important example of this.

The major aim of this book has been to place the public problems of the city in a locational context. Hopefully this has been accomplished. Additional summary comments on the preparation of the book, however, seem appropriate.

First, in considering existing arguments on the public problems of the city it became evident that unsatisfactory conceptualization was responsible for much of their transparency: the absence of a conceptual framework or the use of one lacking rigor, relevance or exhaustiveness were common. In attempting to remedy this the author became aware of the writings of economists on issues of public choice. Consequently this approach has been applied to the analysis of the problems considered in this book. Clearly if its use is as illuminating to others as it has been to the author, further research along these lines seems merited.

Second, in considering public problems where gross inequities are apparent and where publicists are all too willing to supply oversimplified interpretations it is tempting to pursue an argument beyond the limits of available evidence. I have tried to resist these temptations and to consider the questions in the context of all available data. While this may occasionally make for unideological conclusions, perhaps this is the direction in which future research will lead us. At the least it poses a challenge for continuing research in a content area which is both intellectually intriguing and of great public concern.

Selected Bibliography

Advisory Commission on Intergovernmental Relations, *Fiscal Balance in the American Federal System Vol. 2, Metropolitan Fiscal Disparities,* Washington, D.C.: U.S. Government Printing Office, 1967.

Altshuler, A. A., *Community Control,* New York: Pegasus, 1970.

Bish, R. L., *The Public Economy of Metropolitan Areas,* Chicago: Markham, 1971.

Crecine, J. P. (ed.), *Financing the Metropolis,* Beverly Hills: Sage Publications, Inc., 1970.

Chinitz, B. (ed.), *City and Suburb,* Englewood Cliffs: Prentice-Hall, 1964.

Danielson, M. N., *Metropolitan Politics: A Reader,* Boston: Little, Brown and Company, 1971.

Davis, O. A. and A. Whinston, "Economic Problems in Urban Renewal," in E. S. Phelps (ed.), *Private Wants and Public Needs,* New York: W. W. Norton, 1965.

Gordon, D. M. (ed.), *Problems in Political Economy: An Urban Perspective,* Lexington, Mass.: D. C. Heath, 1971.

Guthrie, J. W. et al., *Schools and Inequality,* Cambridge, Mass.: M.I.T. Press, 1971.

Harvey, D. W., "Social Processes, Spatial Form and the Redistribution of Real Income in an Urban System," in M. Chisholm, A. Frey and P. Haggett (eds.), *Regional Forecasting,* London: Butterworth, 1971.

Hearings Before the Select Committee on Equal Educational Opportunity of the U.S. Senate, 91st Congress, 2nd Session on Equal Educational Opportunity: Part 5—De Facto Segregation and Housing Discrimination; Part 6—Racial Imbalance in Urban Schools; Part 7—Inequality of Economic Resources.

Margolis, J. (ed.), *The Analysis of Public Output,* New York: National Bureau of Economic Research, 1970.

Netzer, D., *Economics and Urban Problems,* New York: Basic Books, 1970.

Pascal, A. D. (ed.), *Thinking About Cities,* Belmont, Calif.: Dickenson Publishing Company, 1970.

Perloff, H. and L. Wingo (eds.), *Issues in Urban Economics,* Baltimore: Johns Hopkins Press, 1968.

Rothenberg, J., *Economic Evaluation of Urban Renewal,* Washington, D.C.: Brookings Institution, 1967.

Sexton, P. C., *Education and Income,* New York: Viking Press, 1969.

Sternlieb, G., *The Tenement Landlord,* New Brunswick, N.J.: Rutgers University Press, 1966.

Wolf, E. P. and C. N. Lebeaux, *Change and Renewal in an Urban Community,* New York: Praeger, 1969.